DEMONS

A Biblically
Based Perspective

DEMONS

A Biblically
Based Perspective

Alex Konya

REGULAR BAPTIST PRESS
1300 North Meacham Road
Schaumburg, Illinois 60173–4806

Library of Congress Cataloging-in-Publication Data

Konya, Alex W., 1952—
Demons : a biblically based perspective / Alex W. Konya, Jr.
     p.   cm.
Includes bibliographical references.
ISBN 0-87227-143-9
  1. Demonology—Controversial literature. 2. Demoniac pos-
session—United States—Controversial literature. 3. Exorcism—
Controversial literature. I. Title.
  BT975.K65 1990
  235'.4—dc20   90-33207
                                                            CIP

DEMONS: A BIBLICALLY BASED PERSPECTIVE
© 1990
Regular Baptist Press
Schaumburg, Illinois
Printed in U.S.A. All rights reserved.

Third printing—1997

DEDICATION

To
PAM
my wonderful wife
and our three children
ANN, ALEX and PHILIP

CONTENTS

ACKNOWLEDGMENTS

No work of this kind is possible without the help of some very special people. I therefore wish to express my gratitude to the following people who helped me complete this volume:

My wife, Pam, and my children, who encouraged me and patiently accepted the extra hours of labor.

Dr. John C. Whitcomb, former professor of theology at Grace Theological Seminary, and Dr. Charles R. Smith, vice president and dean of the Master's Seminary, who advised me in the preparation of the thesis that formed the background for this book, read various manuscripts and made many helpful suggestions.

Dr. Robert Gromacki, professor of Bible at Cedarville College; Dr. Terry Zebulske, associate professor at Baptist Bible College; and Dr. Thomas N. Davis, academic dean at Word of Life Bible Institute, who wrote letters on my behalf and made other helpful suggestions.

My parents, Alex and Evelyn Konya, who have encouraged me over the years for such a time as this.

The congregation of the Mayflower Baptist Church, whose prayers and encouragement were invaluable.

Church secretary Janie Tarwacki, who typed the manuscript in its various forms.

Norman A. Olson, book editor at Regular Baptist Press, who offered help and valuable suggestions in the editing and publication process.

FOREWORD

As the western world sinks deeper and deeper into moral chaos and spiritual darkness, many of God's people are asking serious questions about the power of Satan and his demonic hordes. Alex Konya, a graduate of Grace Theological Seminary, and a faithful pastor, has searched the Word of God for several years to discover God's perspective on the power structure of our invisible enemies and how Christians are to deal effectively with it.

Among the questions Pastor Konya Biblically and convincingly answers are these:

How can demon-possession be clearly demonstrated in *any* human being?

Should we *talk* to a demon inside of someone?

If not, do demons *hide* in a person so that no one can discern their presence?

Are any of *our sins* caused by demons?

Were demon-possessed people in New Testament times *especially* wicked?

Why did *the Lord Jesus* and *His apostles* cast out demons?

How could *unbelievers* in New Testament times seem to cast out demons (Matt. 7:21–23; 12:27; Acts 19:13–16)?

Does the New Testament indicate that no one *today* can cast out demons?

What do the New Testament *church epistles* teach us about exorcism?

What did Paul mean by the gift of "discerning of spirits" (1 Cor. 12:10), and John by his command to "test the spirits" (1 John 4:1–3)?

What is our final strategy and resource with regard to Satan and his demons?

If you, as a Christian, cannot answer questions like these, you will find this book to be of great help. Through reading it I have gained a new appreciation for God's marvelous provisions for spiritual victory in our daily walk with Christ our Saviour and

Lord. As the author emphatically reminds us, the New Testament epistles say *nothing* about attacking Satan's empire of darkness or identifying, confronting or casting out demons. But they have much to say about our eternal *position* in Christ through faith and our moment-by-moment *privilege* of putting on the whole armor of God and standing in His strength and authority in the evil day (Eph. 6:13; cf. Rom. 13:12, 14; 1 Pet. 5:8, 9; James 4:7).

Here is an excellent and timely handbook for God's servants to remind us of what God has written "for our instruction, upon whom the ends of the ages have come" (1 Cor. 10:11).

John C. Whitcomb, Th. D.

INTRODUCTION
WHERE DO WE GO FROM HERE?

The year 1973 was not a very good one. America was deeply divided over the continuing war in Vietnam. The presidency was being threatened by a scandal called "Watergate." Spiro T. Agnew resigned the vice presidency in disgrace. Gerald Ford, the man who replaced him, would be president within a year. The nation was seemingly overtaken by illicit drugs and immorality and was coming apart at the seams.

Into the midst of this political and moral maelstrom came a "blockbuster" Hollywood movie. Millions of people flocked to the local cinema and sat transfixed as they watched a twelve-year-old girl snarl, vomit and shout obscenities during a simulated bout with demon possession. The name of the girl was Regan and the film was called *The Exorcist*, based upon the novel of the same name written by William Peter Blatty. The heroes in *The Exorcist* are two Catholic priests who performed the rite of exorcism on the girl, delivering her from demon possession. Since its release in 1973, *The Exorcist* has grossed more than $89 million, and it has become more popular than such films as *The Sound of Music*, *Superman* and *Rocky*.

It seems that with the release of *The Exorcist*, Americans began to exhibit a fresh fascination with the occult and the demonic—a fascination that has yet to wane. Several key factors have contributed to this preoccupation with the demonic.

First, a spiritual vacuum has been created by a fatal combination of theological liberalism and secular materialism. Theological liberalism undercut the authority of the Bible, disallowed the deity of Christ and denied the realities of true forgiveness of sin and eternal life through His substitutionary atonement. This left many without hope or absolutes. Spiritually starved people then looked to secular materialism and technology to find satisfaction in life and to solve their problems, but they found that these solutions to life's problems were also bankrupt. The occult was viewed by some as an alternative to this spiritual emptiness.

Second, the movie industry has not only been cashing in on the occult, but it has actively promoted it as well.[1] Films like *Poltergeist*, *The Omen*, *The Prince of Darkness* and *The Believers* have introduced many adults and teens to the terrifying realm of demon possession, satanic sacrifices and occultic rituals.

Rock music has also taken a decidedly occultic turn. We now have "satanic rock," which has introduced the trappings of Satanism to a generation of groping youth.[2] Satanic symbols are used on stage and on the album covers of rock groups with names like "Black Sabbath," "Coven," "Slayer" and "Venom." Even reporter Tom Jarriel said on ABC's 20/20, "The satanic message is clear, both in the album covers and in the lyrics, which are reaching impressionable young minds."[3]

Next, certain parlor games have encouraged an openness to the spirit realm.[4] Many have ignorantly tinkered with a Ouija board or with tarot cards, not realizing that these so-called "harmless games" can actually put the players in contact with demonic spirits. Tipper Gore, a co-founder of the Parents' Music Resource Center, wrote the following about another popular game, Dungeons and Dragons:

> The popular Dungeons and Dragons game has sold eight million sets. The game is based upon occultic plots, images, and characters which players "become" as they play the game. According to Mrs. Pat Pulling, founder of the organization Bothered About Dungeons and Dragons, the game has been linked to nearly fifty teenage suicides and homicides. Pulling's own son killed himself in 1982 after becoming deeply involved in the game through his school's gifted students program. A fellow-player threatened him with a "death curse," and he killed himself in response.[5]

Even more alarming is the open worship of Satan, with its attendant bizarre rights, sexual perversions and ritualistic sacrifices. Satanic cults seem to be on the increase, along with the crimes that are often associated with them, causing increasing concern among law enforcement officials, educators and pastors.

Finally, the New Age movement has begun to create a new openness of attitude toward the spirit realm. Dave Hunt has identified the following nine items as forms of New Age influence: psychotherapy, visualization techniques, Eastern meditation, biofeedback, positive confession, positive or possibility thinking, hypnosis, holistic medicine and many of the modern self-improvement and success/motivation techniques.[6]

Closely connected with the New Age movement is the phenomenon of "channeling." Channeling is somewhat of a modern adaptation of the old spiritualism, in which mediums and clairvoyants would hold séances in attempts to contact the dead.[7] A "channel" is a contemporary name for a medium, someone who claims to have the ability to confer with so-called spirit entities. In California today, one can consult with a "reincarnated spirit" for $10 to $1500 per hour. Many do so each week.[8]

These alarming trends have not failed to impact the Church. A generation ago, encounters with persons who thought they had "demon problems" were relatively rare in our culture. By contrast, it is not unusual today for a Christian school or church to have within its ranks someone who has had prior contact with occultic activities. Increasing numbers of people are concerned about demonic activity and the possibility of possession, and more of these are being met in the counseling room.

The Christian community has reacted with a wide range of responses to all of this. Some, particularly in the charismatic movement, have gone to bizarre extremes, claiming to cast demons out of not only individuals but also local congregations and even church buildings.[9] Conservative evangelicals have rightly condemned such extremes. Many have held that demon possession has been uncommon in our culture, and thus the need to cast demons out of troubled souls is rare.

However, some noteworthy evangelicals have begun to question this view in the light of our culture's dabbling with the occult. In fact, a growing number of pastors and Bible teachers are even claiming that some *believers* are becoming demon possessed in some sense. The brilliant Bible scholar Merrill F. Unger wrote his classic *Biblical Demonology* in 1952. In that most helpful volume, he claimed that believers cannot be possessed from within by demons. He stated, "The believer, we may confidently rest assured, . . . is shielded from the enemy within the gates."[10] Yet in his

1971 book *Demons in the World Today*, Dr. Unger changed his position, stating that his previous interpretation was in error. The reason for this change was due in part to the number of missionaries who challenged his position, as well as his own counseling experiences with so-called demon-possessed believers. He wrote at that time, "The sincere truth seeker must be prepared to revamp his interpretation to bring it into conformity with the facts as they are."[11] Dr. Unger's final book on this subject, *What Demons Can Do to Saints*, was published in 1977. It contained numerous case studies of what he believed were genuinely demon-possessed believers.

More recently, C. Fred Dickason wrote a book titled *Demon Possession and the Christian*. Dr. Dickason is a respected teacher of the Bible, having taught theology and the New Testament for more than twenty-six years. He claims that from 1974 to 1987 he encountered at least 400 cases of demonized believers.[12]

An extensive ministry of counseling the demonically oppressed has also been engaged in by Mark I. Bubeck. Dr. Bubeck has written two best-selling books, *The Adversary* (1975) and *Overcoming the Adversary* (1984). He has stated his conviction that willing possession of individuals by demons is a growing problem and an extremely dangerous situation.[13] He also has related the story of his youngest daughter's demon possession and how he successfully commanded the spirits to leave.[14]

On the other side of this issue is Peter Masters, a Christian writer and pastor of London's Metropolitan Tabernacle (Spurgeon's home church) since 1970. Masters roundly condemns the idea that true demon possession is rampant today and cites what he believes are six Scriptural reasons why demons cannot occupy people at will.[15] He rejects the notion that demons can hide in their victims[16] and dismisses the possibility that any true believer can be demon possessed.[17] He further asserts that addressing demons in *any manner* is expressly forbidden in the Bible[18] and that those who practice such things may in fact be seriously harming the very people they intend to help.[19]

We then come to the question, Who is right? How shall we evaluate the claims of many that they are casting demons out of numbers of hapless victims? Do believers *really* have the authority to cast out demons? Is there indeed a gift of "Biblical exorcism"? Can a person actually be demon possessed and not realize it? How does one deal with a truly possessed person, or is there such a thing? Or to phrase it another way, Where do we go from here?

Fortunately, God has given a substantial amount of reliable information about demon possession and exorcism in His Word. For believers in Jesus Christ who are committed to shaping their lives and thinking patterns according to that Word, this Biblical material *must* form the basis for any answers to these questions.

It is for this reason that this book has been written. It is time to deal thoroughly with the Biblical evidence and to allow divine revelation to interpret experiences. Scripture must determine truth, and if experiences do not fit such truth, they must be reinterpreted.

Accordingly, four basic principles have governed this book. (1) The Scriptures are assumed to be the inspired, inerrant Word of God. Therefore the incidents recorded in the Bible involving the demonic realm are accepted at face value as true and factual. (2) The Scriptures are *fully* sufficient to give us all the information that we need in this area. Since God has given us "all things that pertain unto life and godliness" (2 Pet. 1:3), it is assumed that all we need to know for godly living, *including* dealing with the demonic, is to be found within the pages of Holy Writ. (3) The data shall be confined to the statements of Scripture. Since exorcism involves dealing with a foe that is cunning, deceiving, depraved and unseen, misinterpreting experiences can be a real possibility. These experiences must be measured by a true, objective, totally reliable standard—and the *only* standard that meets these qualifications fully is the Word of God. (4) Disagreement with other believers in the area of demon possession and exorcism is not to be construed in any way as questioning their faith, integrity or love for Christ and His people. Every effort has been made to discuss the issues in a gentlemanly manner.

It is hoped that this book will cause the reader to carefully think through the New Testament passages relating to demon possession and exorcism, to build a system of beliefs founded upon this doctrinal base and then to evaluate the present scene in the light of the Biblical data.

TRANSLITERATION

Whenever possible, Hebrew and Greek words have been transliterated according to the following form:

Greek		Consonants		Vocalization	
α	a	א	'	_ᴛ_	ā
β	b	בּ	b, ḇ	_ _	a
γ	g	גּ	g, g̱	_ :·_	e
δ	d	דּ	d, ḏ	_··_	ē
ε	e	ה	h	_˙··_	ê
ζ	z	ו	w	_·_	i
η	ē	ז	z	_˙·_	î
θ	th	ח	ḥ		
ι	i	ט	ṭ		
κ	k	י	y		
λ	l	כּ	k, ḵ	_ֹ_	o
μ	m	ל	l	_ֹ_	û
ν	n	מ	m	_··_	u
ξ	x	נ	n		
ο	o	ס	s	_:_	( )ᵉ
π	p	ע	'		
ρ	r	פּ	p, p̱		
σ	s	צ	ṣ	_ᴛ:_	( )ᵃ
τ	t	ק	q		
υ	u	ר	r		
φ	ph	שׂ	ś		
χ	ch	שׁ	š		
ψ	ps	תּ	t, ṯ		
ω	ō				
'	h				

18

CHAPTER ONE

DEMON POSSESSION: WHAT IS IT?

A casual survey of some current writers on the subject of demonology is likely to produce bewilderment to a careful reader. In reviewing case studies reported by those involved in deliverance ministries, Rodger K. Bufford listed nearly a score of symptoms cited as possible evidence of demon possession. These symptoms ranged from such bizarre extremes as supernatural strength and the presence of multiple personalities to vague and nebulous symptoms like phantom pain and depression.[1] Because of this and other reasons, Bufford cautions that it is often difficult to distinguish demon possession from other sinful patterns of everyday living.[2]

To complicate matters further, others claim that demons can often hide in their hosts in order to escape detection.[3] Some have even suggested a "confrontational test" may be necessary to determine the presence or absence of wicked spirits in a person.[4]

As already mentioned, the Bible itself provides a wealth of information from which we can draw some clear conclusions. It describes many instances of undisputed demon possession. When these accounts are carefully examined, one finds that true demonic possession was so terrible and extreme that people had little difficulty in identifying it for what it was.

A LOOK AT THE WORDS

God has chosen to give His revelation to us in words. It is a good idea therefore to begin any study of demon possession by looking at the terms that the New Testament uses to describe it. The New Testament uses four primary terms to describe the demonized state: one having (*echōn*) a demon, one who is demonized (*daimonizomai*), one with (*en*) an unclean spirit and one vexed (*ochloumenous*) with an unclean spirit.

One Having a Demon

The most common description of the demonic state in the New Testament is "one having (*echōn*) a demon or unclean spirit." The New Testament uses the term sixteen times for certain: once in Matthew (11:18), four times in Mark (3:30; 5:15; 7:25; 9:17), three times in Luke (4:33; 7:33; 8:27), five times in John (7:20; 8:48, 49, 52; 10:20) and three times in Acts (8:7; 16:16; 19:13). It was the way people in general usually referred to the demonic state in the New Testament era.

Two distinct ideas are presently held regarding what "having a demon" meant. Some understand the term to have come from the Greek religion and philosophy, where a person was understood to be passive in being possessed by evil spirits. The idea is that the possessed person would bear the demon within himself.[5]

Others believe that "having a demon" (*echōn*) pointed especially to the debilitating physical and mental condition that the demonic state caused.[6] This connection is made because *echōn* was commonly used in the New Testament for having diseases or physical problems by which one was afflicted.[7] Inasmuch as physical and mental torture was one of the most observable and marked symptoms that the demonized exhibited, and the demon was regarded as the cause, the phrase "having a demon" was appropriate. Thus, while the idea of bearing a demon within oneself is present in the use of the phrase "having a demon," the idea also includes seeing a demon as the cause of physical or mental suffering on the part of the demonized person. The victim is therefore under the demon's control.

One Who Is Demonized

The word "demonized" (*daimonizomai*) is the next most frequently used term in the New Testament to describe the demonic state. It is used thirteen times in the New Testament: seven times in Matthew (4:24; 8:16, 28, 33; 9:32; 12:22; 15:22), four times in Mark (1:32; 5:15, 16, 18) and once in both Luke (8:36) and John (10:21). The King James Version almost uniformly translates the term "demon possessed." The word "demonized" is rare outside the New Testament, and therefore we must come to an understanding of the word chiefly by seeing how the New Testament used it.

When the New Testament usage of "demonized" is studied, two key concepts seem to stand out: the demon can exercise control and dominion over the victim that apparently cannot be successfully resisted, and it indwells him. With regard to control, it seems that the New Testament speaks of degrees of demonic influence short of control. However, the word "demonized" is never used of such demonic influence that can be resisted. The New Testament does not seem to indicate that all persons mildly influenced or even strongly influenced were considered demonized.[8]

For example, the New Testament teaches that demons can influence people toward involvement in false doctrine (1 Tim. 4:1), immorality (1 Cor. 7; 1 Tim. 4:1–3) and attitudes of jealousy, divisiveness and pride (James 3:13–16). But the New Testament does not classify such persons as "demonized." Rather, demonized persons were seen as dominated and controlled by the demon, who worked his will through the use of his victim. Demons could use the vocal chords of the demonized to speak (Matt. 8:29, 31; Mark 5:7–10) or keep him from speaking (Matt. 12:22), cause blindness (Matt. 12:22), give supernatural physical strength (Mark 5:3; cf. v. 15), promote nakedness (Mark 5:15), force self-mutilation upon the victim (Mark 5:5) or even produce insanity (Luke 8:35). In these cases, the demonized person appears to be unable to successfully resist the demon's malicious control. He is enslaved.[9]

Furthermore, usage indicates that demonized persons were indwelt bodily by at least one demon. The language of demons "entering in," "going out" or being "cast out" is consistently employed with regard to demonized persons (Matt. 8:16, 32; 9:33; 12:22–24; Mark 1:34; 5:8, 13). If these terms suggest anything, they suggest the idea of a demon actually taking up sovereign residence within the body of the demonized person.

This usage of the term "demonized" is often overlooked by writers and counselors today. It is suggested that this word allows for a range of demonic influence from such minimal forms as planting ideas or suggestions to the control commonly known as "demon possession."[10] Nonetheless, the New Testament seems to use this word only in the narrow sense of demon possession. Other forms of influence cannot therefore be properly called demon possession.

It is also helpful to seek to understand this word by looking at its root and form.[11] The participle form of this word, *daimonizomai*, is used twelve times in the New Testament. As Dickason properly observes, this word has three main parts.

> First, there is the root, *daimon*, which indicates the involvement of demons. Second is the causative stem, *iz*, which shows that there is an active cause in this verb. Third is the passive ending, *omenos*. This conveys the passivity of the person described as demonized.
>
> Putting it all together, the participle in its root form means "a demon caused passivity." This indicates control other than that of the person who is demonized; he is regarded as the recipient of the demon's action. In other words, demonization pictures a demon controlling a somewhat passive human.[12]

In summary, the term "demonized" refers to the invasion of a victim's body by a demon (or demons), in which the demon exercises living and sovereign control over the victim, which the victim cannot successfully resist. The elements of indwelling and the inability to resist the demon's will are what make demonization distinct from lesser forms of demonic influence.

One with an Unclean Spirit

The description of the demonized state as being "one with (*en*) an unclean spirit" is used only twice in the New Testament (Mark 1:23; 5:2). This phrase pictures the person as being under the domination or power of a demon.[13] Thus the terms describing demon possession (one with or having an unclean spirit and one demonized) mean nearly the same thing. This can be most clearly seen in the parallel accounts of the episode with the Gadarene demoniac. Matthew twice referred to him as demonized (*daimoni-zomai*, 8:28, 33). Mark saw him as both demonized (5:15–17), and with (*en*) an unclean spirit (5:2). Luke called him demonized (8:36) and one having (*echōn*) a demon (8:27).

One Vexed with Unclean Spirits

The description of a demonized person as "one vexed with unclean spirits" (*ochloumenous*) occurs only in Acts 5:16. While one cannot be as dogmatic about the condition of these people, the miraculous apostolic cure performed on them suggests a demonized state. Furthermore, a word closely related to "vexed" (*enochleō*) is used in similar fashion for demonized people in Luke 6:18. The word was also used in the Apocrypha for one possessed by an evil spirit,[14] and by the Greeks in a general way for being troubled or worried by someone or something.[15] The phrase "vexed by evil spirits" could be understood, then, as "troubled, disturbed . . . tormented by unclean spirits."[16] The emphasis is upon the tormented, miserable condition of the demonized.

LET THE MASTER ILLUSTRATE: MATTHEW 12:43–45

Almost all of the material dealing with the demonized state is the kind that relates historical incidents—giving examples, but not explanations, of demon possession. An exception to this rule can be found, however, in Matthew 12:43–45, where Jesus teaches about demonization in the form of a similitude or illustration, telling about a wandering, seeking and returning demon. The passage reads:

> When the unclean spirit is gone out of a man, he walketh through the dry places, seeking rest, and findeth none. Then he saith, I will return into my house from [which] I came out; and when he is come, he findeth it empty, swept, and garnished. Then goeth he, and taketh with himself seven other spirits more wicked than himself, and they enter in and dwell there: and the last state of that man is worse than the first. Even so shall it be also unto this wicked generation.

Examining the Context

The general occasion for the events of Matthew 12 was Jesus' casting a demon out of a man. This in turn led to denunciations from the Pharisees, ending with Jesus' sober warnings to them of judgment to come. The account of the wandering demon is the last of these warnings, and Jesus was using the issue of exorcism and demonology to illustrate to His generation the fact and nature of their judgment. Thus one would not be surprised to find figurative expressions here, but the teaching is a true and accurate picture of facts relating to the demonic realm.

Examining the Lessons

A careful evaluation of this passage leads to several distinct lessons concerning the demonized state.

The most obvious lesson from this passage is that demonization involves the indwelling of a demon or demons within the body of a human being. The unclean spirit has "gone out of the man," "return(s)" to his "house" and brings others who "enter in" and "dwell there." Clearly the language here speaks of entering the body of the victim, and it pictures one or more demons indwelling a human being. This sort of language is common in New Testament accounts of the casting out of demons.

Another lesson that this passage presents is that demons *desire* indwelling. The possession of human beings is seen as desirable by demons (at least by those who have grown accustomed to it), because the alternative is the "waterless places" that demons must apparently otherwise inhabit. The term "waterless places" is closely related to other similar, highly figurative passages in the Bible (Isa. 13:20, 21; 34:14; Rev. 18:2). This demonic dwelling place has been figuratively understood to mean places that are difficult to stay in for long, or to refer to the demon's homelessness and restlessness.[17] Perhaps it is best to understand the reference as being to a place unfit for human habitation, a place of restlessness and desolation.[18] Possession of a human being is a more pleasant alternative and is, therefore, a good reason why demons desire to possess people. Since this is so, it is reasonable to conclude that, given the opportunity, demons will attempt to inhabit a willing victim.

Jesus' illustration further teaches the lesson that even though demons desire possession, it is not as easy as man often assumes it to be. The key phrase here is that demons are "seeking rest, and finding none." The word chosen here for "rest" is *anapausin*, and it refers to an "intermission, cessation of any motion, business, labor."[19] It was used, for example, of the rest experienced by traveling foot soldiers.[20] It stands in contrast to another word for rest (*anesis*), which refers only to relaxation, whereas *anapausin* primarily denotes rest from laborious work.[21] So, then, the demon is seeking rest or a pause from some kind of labor. The implication must be that his labor involves finding a willing person who will permit his entrance and that he cannot easily find such a victim.

This fact is rather remarkable in the light of some current opinions concerning demon possession. Some believe that demons can take control of people in droves, whether those people like it or not, or resist them or not. But it appears from Jesus' statement here that the possession of individuals is certainly abnormal or atypical, and demons may have a hard time finding victims.

Yet another interesting and important lesson learned from this passage is that demons may of their own will go out from and return to indwell their victims. Demons may leave their victims (if only temporarily at times) to deceive, to excite fear and dread,[22] or even to promote false religions and unbiblical ministries. For this reason, one cannot argue that all exorcism ministries are Biblically valid simply because they *look* successful. This fact also gives a logical answer for the apparent success of exorcisms conducted in pagan rites, by unbelievers or by those involved in serious doctrinal error. The "exorcisms" are in reality the *voluntary* departure of demons from their victims. This fact alone undercuts the validity of experience as a legitimate way to discover truth concerning demon possession and exorcism.

A final noteworthy lesson from this passage is that those who were once demonized, but now are not, are particularly susceptible to renewed demonic invasion if they are not in a proper spiritual condition. In the illustration, Jesus speaks of one from whom the demon had left, but his life (house) was empty. The demon brings "seven other spirits more wicked than himself," and they "enter in, and dwell there." The result is that the man's "last state" is "worse than the first." Clearly, degrees of severity in demonization exist, depending on the number, power, viciousness and depravity of the indwelling demons.[23] Particularly those who have previous demonic experience must be on guard against giving demons an opportunity to return.

HOW A POSSESSED PERSON ACTS

Perhaps the most striking feature of demon possession in the New Testament is that it is only indirectly connected with gross immorality or moral wickedness. While some contend that demon possession was usually a result of grievous sins of the flesh, or even persistent, rebellious indulgence in sins of the spirit,[24] the New Testament nowhere pictures the demonized as having been unusually wicked people.[25] Instead, they suffer various physical and mental torments that form the *most emphatic* trait of demon possession in the Bible. This can easily be seen from even a casual look at the effect of demonization on its victims, which included such terrible things as wildness of character (Matt. 8:28), violence toward others (Matt. 8:28), dumbness (Mark 9:17; Luke 11:14), deafness (Mark 9:25), screaming or crying out (Mark 1:23, 26; 5:5), self-mutilation (Mark 5:5; 9:22), convulsive seizures (Mark 9:18, 20), general torment (Luke 6:18; Acts 5:16) and even nakedness (Luke 8:27). Nakedness should not here be regarded as primarily an immoral act, but rather as a demonic form of torture. The nakedness seems to be constant and to have lasted for some length of time. Given the fact that in Palestine the difference in temperatures between day and night is considerable in all seasons, the demonized man must have experienced much physical discomfort.

From the prominence of torment in cases of New Testament demon possession, one can conclude that a major reason demons invaded people may have been simply to destroy or to bring misery to their victims.[26] For this reason, severe cases of possession can be expected to involve real human suffering in any cultural situation.

A Different Personality

Also involved in Biblical demon possession is the manifestation of a clearly different personality, the human personality being placed in submission to an alien personality that uses the physical body of the victim to express itself. The voice may at times have been sufficiently "other" that people recognized the demon was speaking through the person.

This manifestation of a demonic personality differs from so-called mental illness in at least two particulars: rationality and relationship. Whenever demons spoke through a person, they always spoke in a rational, logical manner. They spoke with purpose of meaning, having the ability to carry on real discussions. This contrasts sharply with such mentally ill persons as schizophrenics, who speak in such things as "word salads" and irrationalities that simply do not make sense.[27] The gospel narratives show that reality relationships clearly existed for the demons. A clinical psychologist testified:

> The spirits had an ego identification—they knew themselves and they knew who Christ was. There was a literal two-way conversation and relationship in process. In contradistinction, those referred to us as supposedly demon-possessed suffer from a loss of object reality. The voices they hear are schizophrenic hallucinations, attempts to relate once again to the external world from which they have drawn away. . . . This phenomenon is not found at all in the biblical descriptions of demon possession.[28]

Supernatural Knowledge

A final New Testament mark of the demonized state is the display of supernatural knowledge, or as some term it, clairvoyance. This means that the invading demon has supernatural power to know things that people do not normally have the ability to know, and to reveal them. This characteristic is shown in the New Testament by the ability of the demonized to recognize Jesus immediately without being told who He was (Mark 1:24, 34; 3:11, 12; 5:6, 7) and to recognize the ministry of Paul (Acts 16:17; 19:15). The ability to foretell future or secret events was also involved (Acts 16:16).[29]

HOW IT COULD HAPPEN

A remarkable feature of New Testament descriptions of demon possession is that demonized persons were never rebuked or up-braided for being in that condition. With a deep understanding of the lives of men and the facts of disease, Christ at times pointed out a connection between the sick and their sins. This was true of both the man sick of palsy (Matt. 9:2) and the man at the pool of Bethesda (John 5:14). But Christ never once hinted that the demonized were monsters of iniquity, who were receiving the due reward of their deeds. Christ delivered them of His own accord, dismissing them without rebuke.[30] Furthermore, even children were at times demonized (Matt. 17:15; Mark 7:26–30). How could they have been hardened sinners? This Biblical picture stands in stark contrast to some modern authors, who claim that demon-possessed people can get that way through deliberate, persistent indulgence in sins of the flesh or spirit.[31] We are told that people who do not surrender their lives completely to God can open themselves up to demonic invasion.[32] Some assert that demons can invade people who have areas of their lives that are not fully under God's control.[33] Others claim that voluntary yielding to temptation and sin may weaken the human will and make it susceptible to possession.[34] Demons are said to be able to enter a person through the use of drugs or alcohol.[35] Even exposing oneself as a child in a game of "doctor and patient" is said to open the way for an invasion of demons.[36] Such assertions are obviously at odds with the Scriptural data and must be seriously questioned.

Keep Yourselves from Idols

A few hints, however, may point to avenues leading to possible demon possession. One avenue hinted at is idolatry. The Bible gives three lines of proof to suggest this. First, the Old Testament established a link between demons and idolatry. Two passages provide this link. Deuteronomy 32:17 states that, "They sacrificed unto devils [demons], not to God; to gods whom they knew not, to new gods that came newly up, whom your fathers feared not." The term "demons" here is from the Hebrew *šēdîm*, which is generally recognized as a loan word from Akkadian meaning a protecting spirit or demon.[37] Using the same Hebrew term, the psalmist said, "And they served their idols: which were a snare unto them. Yea, they sacrificed their sons and their daughters unto devils [demons]" (Ps. 106:36, 37).

Second, the New Testament also links idolatry with demonism. The Corinthian believers had a number of questions in the area of Christian liberty relating to meat offered to idols. In giving them instruction, Paul warned them against partaking of pagan idol sacrifices. He stated in 1 Corinthians 10:20 and 21:

> But I say, that the things which the Gentiles sacrifice, they sacrifice to devils [demons], and not to God: and I would not that ye should have fellowship with devils [demons]. Ye cannot drink the cup of the Lord, and the cup of devils [demons]: ye cannot be partakers of the Lord's table, and of the table of devils [demons].

Thus both Testaments teach that sacrifice to idols is sacrifice to demons.

Third, a definite geographical relationship linked the bulk of the New Testament examples of demon possession with paganism, characterized by idolatry. It is revealing that nearly all of the New Testament accounts of exorcisms are in geographical locations where the influence of paganism was great. Most of these exorcisms took place in Galilee. The Syrophoenician woman came from farther away. The Bible also makes general references to people coming to Jesus from Syria, Decapolis, Tyre and Sidon, Judaea, beyond the Jordan and Idumea and Jerusalem. These general references, which may have referred to general healing as well as exorcism, are the only ones that suggest the presence of any numbers of demonized people in the area of Jerusalem. In fact, the only definite reference to demon possession in connection with Jerusalem is found in Peter's exorcisms recorded in Acts 5:16. John, whose Gospel centers uniquely upon Jerusalem, mentions no cases of demon possession. Further references to demon possession in Acts list demonized people as living in Samaria, Philippi and Ephesus. While not conclusive, this evidence does suggest that demon possession was particularly prevalent in pagan areas, where idolatry was more common.[38]

Involvement with the Occult

Another avenue that apparently opens a door to the demonized state is occultic involvement. Two examples of this are given in Acts. In Acts 16:16, a demonized girl is said to have a "spirit of divination," literally a "spirit, a Python." The name came from the ancient occultic oracle at Delphi, or Pytho, as the city was also called. Soothsayers were therefore called "Pythons." Inasmuch as this woman was such a soothsayer, a strong connection exists between demonization and magic or sorcery.[39]

Acts 19:8–20 gives another example of the link between demonization and the occult. Here, Paul performed an unusually great number of miracles and exorcisms in Ephesus (19:11, 12) and even was confronted with false exorcists (19:13–16). It is no accident that the great number of exorcisms were performed in a significant occultic center, for which Ephesus was noted in ancient times. The city was particularly famous for its magical scrolls that contained special spells. Magical parchments were accordingly called "Ephesian Scripts."[40] When many Ephesians came to Christ, they burned their occultic literature, which Luke valued at over fifty thousand drachmae (probably worth over a million dollars by modern standards; Acts 19:19).

In the light of the above facts, it is unsurprising that missionaries and others who minister to those intimately involved with idolatrous cultures, or people entrenched in occultic practices, report the bulk of modern cases of demonization. From the New Testament data, one would expect that such situations would be more likely to lead to the demonized state. In this culture, the most likely places where true demon possession may be encountered could be with persons who have been involved in Satanism or the occult, or persons who come from other cultures with idolatrous backgrounds. The combination of occultic fascination and the influx of such idolatrous cultural ideas as Eastern mysticism may contribute to an increase in cases of demon possession in America.

However, caution must be exercised even here. The Canaanite culture that God commanded Old Testament Israel to destroy was rife with occultic and idolatrous practices. Their horrible practices included child sacrifices, the worship of demonic deities, gross sexual perversions and occultic activities such as spiritism, astrology and consulting the dead. Israel, to its shame, ignored God's warnings and practiced all of these things. Yet the Old Testament contains no instruction concerning demon possession or exorcism, and the Old Testament presents no clear-cut example of demon possession.[41] This reticence of the Scriptures should serve as a warning for all to heed. Even *extensive* involvement with the occult or idolatry does not guarantee demon possession on the part of those who have been so involved.

RECOGNIZING DEMON POSSESSION

One of the real difficulties in dealing with the demon possessed centers around the perplexing question of recognition. Exactly how does one know whether a person is demonized or not? Surprisingly, no such problem seemed to exist in the Gospels or Acts. Not only Jesus and the apostles, but even pagans were able at times to recognize a demonized person. Two outstanding examples of this can be seen in the Syrophoenician woman (Mark 7:24–30) and the man whose son suffered from demonic epilepsy (Mark 9:14–29; cf. Matt. 17:14–20). Both persons correctly diagnosed the problems that their children had as being due to demon possession. In other instances, demoniacs were brought to Jesus to be delivered (Mark 1:32–34; Acts 5:16; Matt. 9:32–34), and these passages show that a clear distinction was made between simple disease and demonization. It is truly amazing that no one in the New Testament ever disagreed about the presence of demons in a specific case of possession.[42] How did they know?

The symptoms of bodily possession mentioned earlier in this book show true demonization to be so dreadful and so evident that only a little perception was needed to recognize the problem and its difference from simple mental illness.[43] It did not take a spiritual person to recognize the problem, because it was so severe.[44]

In contrast, many believe that a person can be demonized, and yet nobody may be able to recognize it. These demonized persons are said to sometimes live normal, moral and exemplary lives, which would not generally cause one to suspect a demonic state.[45] Or, demons may "hide" in their victims, merging their personalities into the personalities of their victims. It is claimed that in such cases, the physical symptoms of actual demonization may occur if the demons are challenged with expulsion.[46] However, these statements provoke this question: If no obvious symptoms of demonization occur in a person, how does one know to challenge the demons with expulsion? *The New Testament accounts never picture "secret" demonization!* People were assumed to be free of demons unless they displayed the obvious symptoms of possession mentioned earlier. According to the New Testament accounts, only such were dealt with by Jesus and the apostles.

SUMMARY

The Biblical words for demon possession give a frightful picture of true demon possession. It involves a demon or demons indwelling a person's body, with the demon exercising living and sovereign control over his victim, which cannot be successfully resisted. These features of demonic indwelling and control distinguish demonization from lesser forms of demonic influence.

Jesus' illustration in Matthew 12:43–45 clearly shows that demons desire to indwell persons. The possession of a victim is more difficult, however, than many assume. Once a demon has indwelt a person, he may also leave voluntarily. This fact should cause believers to be careful about accepting the validity of exorcism experiences based upon results alone.

The primary characteristic of demon possession in the New Testament was physical and mental torment. Other marks of possession were the display of another rational, self-conscious personality and clairvoyance. Since the symptoms of demonization were so obvious and unique, no "tests" were employed to determine whether a person was demonized. Even unbelievers could often correctly recognize the condition. People were not assumed to be demonized unless the condition was obvious.

The responsibility of the demonized for their plight is not emphasized in the New Testament. It does hint, however, that idolatry and occultic involvement may open the door to demon possession. This may help to provide an explanation for the greater number of reports of possession related by missionaries serving in idolatrous or occultic cultures, as well as the increase in reports of possession in this country. However, even involvement with the occult or idolatry does not guarantee demon possession.

CHAPTER TWO

JESUS CHRIST: DELIVERER FROM THE DEMONIC

I n the ministry of our Lord on this earth, casting out demons occupied an important and marvelous position. Multitudes were freed from the terrible effects of demon possession, and the Son of God was magnified. The accounts of these events seem simple enough; yet there are those who deny the reality of these wonderful miracles.

THE CRY OF THE SKEPTICS

There have always been those who have voiced skepticism toward the Jesus of the Bible. They have questioned His very historicity, His miracles, His words, His substitutionary atonement, His resurrection and His return. It is no wonder, then, that attacks have been made upon the authenticity of Jesus' work of casting out demons.

Those who deny that Jesus cast out demons argue for their position from three standpoints. Some claim Jesus knew that the demonized were really only diseased, but He accommodated Himself to the superstition of His contemporaries. Others argue that, due to the self-emptying of Christ referred to in Philippians 2:7, His limitations included being bound to some of the erroneous traditions of His time. He thus incorrectly believed in the existence of demons. Still others claim that Jesus never did teach the reality of demons and that He did not cast them out. Rather, they claim the casting out to be part of a later tradition, which is preserved in the gospel records.

Falsehood Number One: Jesus Was an Accommodator

Those who propose the accommodation theory state that Christ and His apostles, when they referred to demonization, spoke that way in order to deal with the common people on their own terms. In other words, they "accommodated" their teaching to the superstitions of their hearers, without ever claiming that the idea of demon possession was true or false.[1] Some say that this was done for the purest of motives; namely, that Jesus entered into the superstition of those who thought they were demonized, pretending to "free" them, so that they would feel better and once again live normal, happy lives.[2]

The chief problem with this idea is a moral one. Even if Jesus Christ accommodated these superstitions for the purest of motives, He would have been guilty of deliberately misrepresenting the truth and supporting a most destructive and damaging superstition. Superstitions about demons pervaded Jewish culture in the time of our Lord and bound the populace in fear and dread. How could Jesus Christ willingly contribute to an unfounded fear that held many in real bondage, and still maintain His integrity? A *holy* Son of God would by nature be incapable of such a deliberate lie. Furthermore, New Testament demonization was *not* mere superstition!

Falsehood Number Two: Jesus Was Ignorant

Others have clearly understood the theological implications of the accommodation theory and believe in the full deity of Christ. Yet they claim to see close parallels between the false religious ideas of Jesus' day concerning exorcism, and Jesus' teaching and actions on the subject. In order to reconcile these seemingly contradictory concepts, they have suggested that, due to Jesus' self-emptying in His incarnation, Jesus accepted the limitations of first-century knowledge, including their superstitions regarding exorcism.[3] In other words, a part of our Lord's becoming man included His being bound in some ways to the superstitions of His contemporaries.

This view has three problems. First, Jesus' teaching and actions do *not* correspond with the teachings of His day. When one reads a summary of the ideas about demonism prevalent in Jesus' day, and then reads the Biblical accounts concerning Jesus' actions and words on the subject, he is astounded at the simplicity and reserve in Jesus' ministry as Jesus dealt with demonism.

Second, if Jesus had been truly enslaved to His times, He would have showed that subjection in other superstitions or false religious beliefs of His day.[4] Jesus' confrontation with contemporary religious leaders over their oral law and superstitions is a dominant theme in the Gospels. Jesus' teachings in general were *radically* different from those of most of His contemporaries in many other areas besides demonism. He clearly showed that He *was* able to reject the popular traditions of His times.

Third, if Jesus' self-emptying resulted in His teaching false doctrine, it completely undermines any understanding of His ministry as authoritative. If Jesus could not be trusted in this point, how could He be trusted in *any* point? If Jesus was deceived in the area of demonism, what guarantee does one have that He was not also deceived in the meaning of His death? Or to put it another way, if we cannot trust Jesus' words about demonization, how can we trust His words in John 3:16? In no case was Jesus' "limited" knowledge (due to His self-emptying) also erroneous knowledge. Limited knowledge does not need to be erroneous knowledge.

Falsehood Number Three: The Bible Is Untrustworthy

According to the third concept, the "teachings of Jesus" recorded in the Gospels are not His at all—they are the additions of other writers. The language of demon possession was the writers' way of explaining the unknown causes that produced what were then looked upon as unusually strange symptoms and manifestations of what we know today to be diseases.[5] Or, the Gospels are records of the *traditions* concerning Jesus' activities that developed years later, not the historical facts.[6] These ideas must be rejected as inconsistent with the Biblical doctrine of the inspiration of Scripture. The Scriptures claim that the Bible is the product of the actual creative breath of God (2 Tim. 3:16), and that it was written by holy men of God who were specially superintended by the Holy Spirit to guard them from error (2 Pet. 1:21). The gospel records are thus more than traditions; they are the very Word of God.

JESUS WAS NOT AN EXORCIST

What is an exorcist? The word "exorcist" (*exorkistēs*) is closely related to the Greek verb *exorkizō*. The root meaning of *exorkizō* is "to adjure, charge under oath."[7] This word was used only once in the New Testament (Matt. 26:63) when the Jewish ruling body charged Jesus under oath to answer them properly. Apparently, from the idea of adjuration in general, the word developed a technical sense of adjuring and charging demons to leave their victims. Hence the word "exorcist" (*exorkistēs*) became connected with casting out demons by means of adjuration, incantations or religious or solemn ceremonies.[8] It referred to the performing of certain rites, almost always including the use of charms and incantations, as well as the invocation of a reputedly holy name and magical formulas.[9] It is in this sense that the term "exorcist" is used in its only instance in the New Testament, Acts 19:13, where false Jewish exorcists stand in view.

The Jewish historian Josephus gives a typical illustration of the methods of exorcists in Jesus' day. He mentions one Eleazar, who was said to perform exorcisms in the presence of the Roman emperor Vespasian. The "cure" that Eleazar used was this: He put ". . . a ring that had a root of one of those sorts mentioned by Solomon" to the nostrils of the demoniac and allegedly drew the demon out through the nostrils, while adjuring the demon never to return again. The "proof" that the demon had left was seen when a cup that the exorcist had set some distance away was overturned by the "departing spirit"![10]

Jesus' simple, dignified, yet totally effective method of dealing with demons stands in sharp contrast to these elaborate rituals. In fact, the New Testament writers seemed to have deliberately avoided using *exorkistēs* to describe Jesus' ministry of casting out demons.[11] It is thus correct to say that the Gospels technically do not contain a single case of exorcism proper by Jesus, and for the sake of accuracy, Jesus should not be considered an exorcist.

This striking lack of ritual or incantation in the ministry of Jesus to the demonized was a matter of constant amazement to those who watched. Many of them had seen contemporary exorcists in action, but Jesus' methods were radically different. The reaction of the crowd in Mark 1:27 is typical: "And they were all amazed, insomuch that they questioned among themselves, saying, What is this? A new teaching! For with authority he commandeth even the unclean spirits, and they obey him."[12] In another instance, the multitudes marveled, saying, "It was never so seen in Israel" (Matt. 9:32, 33).

HOW THE MASTER DID IT

Jesus' deliverance of the demon possessed varied in its methods. In most cases, He cast out the demons with a mere word (Matt. 8:16), or He rebuked them (Mark 1:25, 26). But on at least one occasion He simply pronounced a girl delivered, though she had never had direct contact with Jesus (Mark 7:29). Normally, He forbade demons to speak (Mark 1:34; Luke 4:41); but at least once He not only carried on a dialogue with a demon, but He also asked him his name (Mark 5:1–13). Usually, the faith of the demonized or their friends was inconsequential as far as the Gospel records were concerned; but in at least one instance, the faith of a mother was involved in the deliverance of her daughter (Matt. 15:28). Whatever simple but varied method Jesus used, deliverance was always complete and instantaneous. The New Testament gives no records of gradual deliverance or protracted prayer meetings in connection with the ministries of either Jesus or the apostles.

This fact creates two serious problems for those who claim that believers today are authorized to cast out demons as Jesus did. First, what method should be used? Proponents must admit that Jesus used no standard technique, and yet they must follow some kind of pattern in casting out demons. They therefore often resort to a "pick-and-choose" system, where certain elements of Jesus' ministry are picked out as an example. This decision is usually based upon experience and results.

For example, many advocates of present-day deliverance ministries stress the importance of casting out demons by name. One wrote:

Severely demonized people often have many demons controlling them. All these demons have names, and their names can
be demanded by an accredited representative of Jesus, as Jesus
Himself demanded them. The evil spirit can also be cast out of
its victim by the use of its name by the accredited representative
of Jesus, as Jesus Himself did. This phenomenon did not occur
only in Jesus' day. It is a common procedure today where prayer
battles are conducted for the release of the demonized. I can
personally attest, as the witness of similar releases, how important it is to confront the demon by name.[13]

Some mention the following as possible ingredients of deliverance from demons: the need to command the demons never to
return, based upon Mark 9:25;[14] the importance of looking the
victim in the eye;[15] prayer;[16] and even the use of Christian music.[17]
Still others flatly state that Jesus used no particular technique.[18]
Since the Bible offers no consistent pattern or teaching regarding
how to cast out demons, suggestions are sometimes given to use
whatever works—including a Roman Catholic ritual or suggestions from an Anglican publication.[19]

The fact is, Jesus' methods were never meant to be used as
patterns to be followed by believers of any age. Their diversity and
uniqueness strongly suggest the unique authority of the Son of
God, as will be demonstrated later.

A second problem that advocates of present-day exorcism
ministries must wrestle with is the admitted failure of modern
exorcists to bring about immediately the full deliverance of
victims from demon possession. Often, deliverance from demonization is a protracted struggle, and even after days, weeks or
months, full deliverance is not achieved.[20] This practice stands in
stark contrast to the consistent, immediate and full deliverances
that Jesus always brought about. This failure of modern exorcists
speaks eloquently to the fact that they are not casting out demons
as Jesus did. Theirs is a different phenomenon.

WHAT IT ALL MEANT

The deliverance of the demonized was a compassionate,
loving ministry that Jesus exercised. We cannot possibly imagine
the sense of relief, release and joy that the formerly possessed must

have experienced as our Lord graciously and immediately delivered them. One should not minimize this demonstration of love and compassion to these hapless victims of a cruel enemy. However, Jesus' deliverance of the demon possessed had other great implications as well.

These Were Special Miracles

What is a miracle? How can it be defined? When the miracles of the New Testament are carefully examined, a threefold picture emerges. One theologian has well summarized this picture,[21] defining a miracle as (1) an extraordinary event that cannot be explained in terms of ordinary natural forces; (2) an event that causes the observers to suggest a superhuman personal cause; and (3) an event that gives evidence of implications much wider than the event itself.

Did Jesus' casting out of demons meet these criteria? An examination of the passages involved shows that it did. The fact that they were extraordinary events can be clearly seen by the reactions of the people who witnessed them. The common response of the crowd was to marvel (Matt. 9:33; Mark 1:27; 5:20; Luke 11:14) and to be astonished (Luke 9:43). The word "marvel" (*thaumazō*) was a commonly used term to designate a miracle. They also exclaimed, "It was never so seen in Israel" (Matt. 9:33). This statement is remarkable when one considers the fact that the Jews were familiar with exorcism and that exorcists were a fairly common sight (Luke 11:19, 20; Acts 19:13, 14). Jesus' expulsions of demons were truly extraordinary and unique, and the people were unable to explain the immediate, full deliverance of victims in terms of ordinary natural forces.

Furthermore, those who observed these events obviously saw that a supernatural, personal cause was behind them. This is most evidently seen in the charge of Jesus' enemies. Even they could not deny the supernatural nature of Jesus' deliverances of the demonic; but they charged on at least two occasions that Jesus acted under the power of Satan (Matt. 9:34; Luke 11:15).

Finally, the demon expulsions of Jesus were understood to have a much wider meaning than merely helping people in need. This fact is demonstrated in Mark 1:27, where the authority that

Jesus showed in casting out demons was unquestionably linked with the authentication of Jesus and His message. The crowd exclaimed, "What is this? A new teaching! For with *authority* he commandeth the unclean spirits, and they obey him." It was thus Jesus' authority over the forces of darkness that the crowds saw as most compelling. It is therefore plain that Jesus' activity in casting out demons fits the threefold criteria for the miraculous mentioned earlier.

Not only could Jesus' casting out demons be classified as miracles, it is also closely connected with miracles of healing. It is inaccurate to say that the demonized state was simply another way of describing various illnesses, and that casting out demons was a different way of stating that a person was healed of disease. An examination of the New Testament shows that a clear difference is often made between simple illness and its healing, in contrast to the demonized state, with its attendant casting out of demons (Matt. 4:24, 25; 9:27–34; 10:1; Mark 1:34; 3:10–12; 6:13; Luke 7:21; 9:1; 13:32; Acts 5:16; 8:7).[22]

However, demons could and did produce illness as well. Not all illnesses were attributed to demons. But inasmuch as physical suffering was a chief characteristic of the demonized state and casting out the demons resulted in physical well-being in these cases, deliverances from demons were also sometimes classified as healings (Matt. 15:28; Acts 5:16; 10:38; 19:11, 12). Diseases arising from natural causes, such as epilepsy, deafness or dumbness, could also be the result of demon possession (Matt. 12:22; 17:15; cf. Luke 9:42). If natural causes brought about the disease, the person was healed by the supernatural removal of those causes and restoration of the body. If demonization was the cause, healing occurred by casting the demon out. Thus casting out demons in the Gospels could also be regarded as a species of healing.[23]

Four distinct lines of proof plainly indicate that demon expulsions were to be regarded as a type of miraculous healing.[24] First, they are called at times "healings" (Matt. 4:24; 12:22; Mark 3:10; Luke 6:19; 7:21; 8:2; Acts 10:38). Second, similar words are used for miraculous healings in general and demon expulsions in particular. Both diseases and demons are rebuked (Mark 1:25; cf. Luke 4:39). Third, at times a similarity in the method of dealing with general illness and demonization took place. Jesus dealt with both diseases and demons simply by the word of authority (Matt. 8:16; cf. Mark 2:10–12); and at times He dealt with both from a distance, with no physical contact involved (Matt. 8:5–13; cf. Mark 7:24–30). Fourth, both demonic expulsions and general healings resulted in similar responses from the onlookers, expressed in similar words. They voiced amazement, accompanied by the exclamation that such things had never before been seen (Mark 2:12; cf. Matt. 9:33).

Not only are Jesus' demon expulsions similar to other miracles of healing, but a remarkable analogy exists between Jesus' deliverance of demoniacs and the calming of the sea during a storm. At the height of the storm Jesus rebuked (*epitiman*) the wind and waves (Mark 4:39), which immediately calmed. Elsewhere in Mark, "rebuke" (*epitimaō*) is regularly used in the context of Jesus rebuking demons, resulting in the deliverance of those who were demonized (Mark 1:25; 3:12; 9:25). This choice of the word "rebuke" in the accounting that Mark gave of the calming of the sea is so unusual and arresting that some have suggested Mark deliberately intended to show a link with demon expulsion.[25] Some commentators have even gone further, flatly stating that Mark was hinting at a demonic source to the storm.[26] It is perhaps better to understand Jesus' rebuke as a giving of personal qualities to the impersonal storm (Ps. 106:9).[27] Yet, a clear link *is* here in the realm of Jesus' supernatural authority. The authority that Jesus displayed in His mastery of the demonic realm (Mark 1:27) was now displayed in His mastery in the realm of nature (Mark 4:41). Another link is thus provided between Jesus' casting out of demons and other miracles, showing that His exorcisms *were*, in fact, a species of miracle—and therefore unique.

These Were Signs of the Kingdom

The demon expulsions performed by Christ were not only seen as miracles, but they also demonstrated to His hearers that He was offering God's kingdom and that He was the Messiah-King. He came to destroy the works of Satan; and His triumph over the demonic realm proved He was Who He claimed to be—the King and Conqueror, Who came to offer that kingdom to Israel.

In Matthew 12:22, Jesus cast a demon out of a deaf and dumb man, healing him. The crowd responded by seeing a unique supernatural authority behind the act, and began to question whether Jesus could indeed be the promised Messiah ("Son of David"; Matt. 12:23). When the Pharisees heard this, however, they charged that the supernatural power behind Jesus' deed was not God's, but Beelzebub's (Matt. 12:24). Jesus answered them by saying,

> Every kingdom divided against itself is brought to desolation; and every city or house divided against itself shall not stand: And if Satan cast out Satan, he is divided against himself; how shall then his kingdom stand? And if I by Beelzebub cast out devils [demons], by whom do your children [sons] cast them out? therefore, they shall be your judges. But if I cast out devils [demons] by the Spirit of God, then the kingdom of God is come unto you. Or else how can one enter into a strong man's house, and spoil his goods, except he first bind the strong man? and then he will spoil his house (Matt. 12:25–29).

An important thought must be considered in this statement: Jesus' casting out of demons by the Holy Spirit was a sign that the kingdom was near. In Jesus' ministry, the people witnessed that power of the age to come already in operation.[28] This was demonstrated in the fact that Jesus' casting out demons amounted to a spoiling and triumphing over Satan's kingdom.[29] In the present passage, the "strong man" and his "house" are prominent. The "strong man" is Satan. This can be seen in the parallel language of Matthew 12:25, where the strong man is Satan and his "house" is his kingdom. Jesus has entered this world, which is Satan's "house" or kingdom (cf. Luke 4:5, 6), and is plundering his "goods" by delivering the persons who were afflicted with demonization by Satan and his demonic hordes. Satan is being bound, while his victims are being freed. Thus Jesus is pictured as the One through Whom the kingdom of Satan is being defeated in preparation for the coming kingdom of God. Jesus' expulsions of demons are a clear sign of His power and authority, affirming that the people were correct in calling Him the Son of David, and that the kingdom of God was near.[30]

Not only was the casting out of demons by Jesus a sign in itself of the coming of the kingdom, but it was also closely linked with the preaching of this kingdom's nearness by both Jesus and His special representatives.[31] Matthew stated:

> And Jesus went about all Galilee, teaching in their synagogues, and preaching the gospel of the kingdom, and healing all manner of sickness and all manner of disease among the people. And his fame went throughout all Syria: and they brought unto him all sick people that were taken with diverse diseases and torments, and those [who] were possessed with devils [demons], and those which were [epileptics], and those who had the palsy; and he healed them (Matt. 4:23–25).

In the parallel account in Mark 1:14 and 15, the gospel of the Kingdom is described. Jesus said, "The time is fulfilled, and the kingdom of God is at hand: repent ye, and believe the gospel." After this summary statement concerning what Jesus taught on the first Galilean tour, Mark gave an account of one day of Jesus' activity in Capernaum. The most prominent features of this activity are Jesus' healing and casting out of demons, both in the synagogue (Mark 1:21–28) and at His door in the evening (Mark 1:32–34).

This close link between Jesus' preaching about the kingdom and casting out demons can also be observed in His commission to the Twelve and the Seventy for their preaching tours. To the Twelve He said, "And as ye go, preach, saying, The kingdom of heaven is at hand. Heal the sick, cleanse the lepers, raise the dead, cast out devils [demons]: freely ye have received, freely give" (Matt. 10:7, 8). Likewise the Seventy were to proclaim, "The kingdom of God is come [near] unto you" (Luke 10:9, 11). Their attesting miracles included the subjection of demons (Luke 10:17, 19).

In all of these instances, the casting out of demons served as a kind of preparation for the coming of the kingdom. Jesus' success, along with that of His representatives, showed that the time was near for Satan's dominion to end and for God to establish His kingdom on earth.[32] These demonic expulsions were thus especially fitting to authenticate the message of the gospel of the kingdom preached by Jesus and His representatives. For this reason they are connected closely with the kingdom message in the Gospels.

The word "rebuke" (*epitimaō*) also provides a close link between Jesus' casting out demons and the coming of God's kingdom. It is used five times in the New Testament in connection with the demon expulsions performed by Jesus (Matt. 17:18; Mark 1:25, 9:25; Luke 4:35; 9:42). It is always translated "rebuke," and can be defined to mean "rebuke, reprove, censure," with a secondary meaning of "speak seriously, warn" in order to prevent an action or bring one to an end.[33] The Old Testament Hebrew word for "rebuke" was *gā'ar*.[34] Of the twenty-eight times this word occurs in the Old Testament, twenty-one texts use *gā'ar* for God's overcoming of His enemies for His purposes. Of special interest are those passages that deal with God's rebuke of the sea to accomplish its restraint (Job 26:11; 2 Sam. 22:15; Ps. 18:15; 104:6, 7; 106:9). This image is sometimes used to describe figuratively God's future goal of defeating His enemies (Isa. 17:13; 50:2; Nah. 1:4).[35] The important factor in all of these passages is that in every case "rebuke" (*gā'ar*) is used to denote God's authoritative word that exercises power over that which stands in the way of the fulfillment of His purpose.[36]

It is particularly meaningful to see in the New Testament the two senses in which "rebuke" (*epitimaō*) is used in connection with Jesus. It is used of His rebuke of the elements (Mark 4:39; cf. Luke 8:24), which recalls God's Old Testament rebuke of the sea. The gospel writers clearly wanted the reader to see in this event the actions of God. Likewise, the authoritative word of rebuke that Jesus used to cast out demons recalls the many Old Testament examples of God's vanquishing of that which opposed Him, to accomplish His purposes.

A further astounding fact is that, whereas the gospel writers commonly used "rebuke" to describe how Jesus cast out demons, no examples of such a use of the word appear in either Jewish or Greek exorcism literature. There is *no* evidence that these exorcisms were thought of as being acts with a wider meaning other than the exaltation of the performer.[37] The conclusion to this seems to be that the gospel writers deliberately chose "rebuke" as a description for Jesus' casting out of demons to show positively that these acts meant something radically different from the exorcisms performed by Greek or Jewish wonder-workers. The term "rebuke" showed that Jesus was Lord over even demons, and that His word alone could vanquish the powers of darkness to prepare for the establishment of His kingdom. Thus the word "rebuke" reveals the unconditional deity and Messiahship of Jesus.

Matthew 11:12 describes a violent struggle in connection with the kingdom. Jesus said, "And from the days of John the Baptist until now the kingdom of heaven suffereth violence, and the violent take it by force." This passage is admittedly difficult; but it seems best to understand this statement as a reference to Satan's struggle with the Messiah at the time when the kingdom of God was at hand. Satan and his demons were engaged in a struggle to maintain the rule and authority that they held over the world and people (cf. Luke 4:5 ff.),[38] seeking to keep the kingdom of God from replacing it. Because of them, the kingdom was being "violently treated," and Satan and his demon hordes were the main "violent ones." The result was shown in clashes that were indeed violent in character, as best demonstrated in Jesus' casting out of demons.

Violence often characterized this clash between Jesus and Satan. In the context of Matthew 11:12, violence marked the death of John the Baptist, who is in view in the previous verses. It also often marked the departure of demons that Jesus cast out (Mark 1:26; 5:13; 9:26), as well as the violent harm that was often inflicted upon the demonized (Mark 5:3 ff.; 9:18, 20, 22).[39]

This violent struggle between Satan's kingdom and the kingdom of God thus offers a possible explanation for the extraordinary number of demonized persons found during the time of Jesus' ministry, and consequently, the great emphasis upon demonic expulsions performed by Jesus and His representatives in this period. John the Baptist's appearance had been a warning to Satan that his kingdom was in serious jeopardy. It accordingly signaled a time of feverish activity for hosts of Satan's powerful and brutal demonic assailants who had as their object the "taking of the kingdom by force"—meaning the destroying of the results of the preaching of John, Jesus and His representatives, thereby keeping mankind in their power.[40] It is truly remarkable that the Bible has no clear records of demonized people in the Old Testament period,[41] and after Calvary the phenomenon again begins to fade[42] until one finds virtually no discussion of demon possession or how to cast out demons in the Epistles. The coming of the King, with Satan's vicious opposition to Him and His kingdom, may explain these facts.

So, then, Matthew 11:12 refers to what happened when the King entered the "house" of the "strong man," and, binding him, plundered his "goods." The link between Jesus, demon expulsions and the offering of the kingdom of God is thus further established.

These Showed the Authority of Our Lord

Jesus' demonic expulsions were not only miracles and kingdom-related signs. They also uniquely demonstrated Jesus' authority over Satan's realm. This truth is demonstrated in the reactions of the demons themselves to Jesus' word of rebuke. It was so common for the demons to react vocally to being cast out that Jesus usually did not permit them to speak (Mark 1:34). But when they did speak, they revealed that (1) they knew His identity (Mark 1:34) as the "Holy One of God" (Mark 1:24), Son of God (Mark 3:11) and Messiah (Mark 3:11); (2) He had power to torment them (Mark 5:7, 8); (3) He could cast them out of the victim and send them to the place of His choice, such as into animals (Mark 5:12, 13) or the abyss (Luke 8:31). These astounding reactions further point to the authoritative nature of demon expulsions by Jesus. They showed that He was Lord over even the realm of demons, and sovereign in His actions when confronted by them.

IMPLICATIONS FOR TODAY

Before continuing, it is fitting to pause for a moment to reflect upon some implications of Jesus' deliverance ministry for the present age. It has been demonstrated that if a single word exists that best summarizes those implications, it is the word "unique."

For one thing, the times were unique. The enormous outbreak of demon possession witnessed during Jesus' era was shown to be no accident; it was strongly related to the mission of Christ. Our

Lord came both to offer the kingdom to Israel and to offer Himself as the perfect sacrifice for sin. To thwart this mission, Satan summoned the forces of darkness for a frontal assault aimed at Jesus and His apostles—an assault that involved violent and extreme measures (Matt 11:12; cf. Mark 1:26; 5:13; 9:17, 18, 20, 22, 26). Satan was about to suffer defeat, and he therefore used all of his power to oppose Christ's kingdom. The incredible amount of demon possession witnessed at that time was an aspect of this cosmic struggle.

It is therefore doubtful that we are presently seeing true demonic possessions in such frequency as they occurred during the era of the Gospels. In fact, the phenomena of demon possession and exorcism seem to begin to diminish sharply even during the lifetime of the apostles (see the next chapter).

Furthermore, this idea is confirmed from other passages of Scripture as well. Colossians 2 flatly states that Christ is the head over all principalities and powers (Col. 2:10). These powers include Satan's evil demonic armies (Eph. 6:12). It also asserts that, through His work at Calvary, Christ defeated these foes (Col. 2:15). He "spoiled" them and made an open display of them in triumph. So, then, judgment has already been pronounced against Satan and his demons; the sentence has only to be executed. And it will be, when Christ establishes His kingdom on earth (Rev. 20:10).

Because Satan and his minions are defeated foes, their power seems presently to be restrained in some ways by God. Second Thessalonians 2:7 declares, "For the secret power of lawlessness is already at work; but the one who now holds it back will continue to do so till he is taken out of the way" (NIV). Regardless of the specific identity that one gives to this "restrainer," it is obvious that God is in some sense restraining the powers of evil in this present age, and the full power of Satan is not permitted to be unleashed. However, during the tribulation period immediately preceding Christ's return, this restraint will be removed. The result will be another unprecedented time of Satanic and demonic activity (2 Thess. 2:8–12; Rev. 9:1–11; 12:7–12; 16:12–14; 18:1, 2). It is no accident that the circumstances of this future outbreak will be similar to the circumstances surrounding Christ's first coming—God's breaking into human history in connection with the establishment of His kingdom. Now this does not imply that Satan and demons are inactive today. The Bible forcefully warns us otherwise (Eph. 6:11–13; James 4:7; 1 Pet. 5:8). Nor does this deny the possibility of demon possession today. It *does* warn us, however, not to use the abundance of demon possessions in the time of Christ as a pattern for our times.

It was pointed out that the *manner* in which Jesus cast out demons was also unique. As the evidence was presented, it was concluded that no clear-cut pattern could be discovered concerning how Jesus handled the demonized. Due to this fact, it is not surprising that such diversity of method exists today among would-be exorcists, who search in vain for such a pattern. The reason no pattern for casting out demons can be found in Jesus' ministry is that no pattern was ever intended! The variety of approaches used by our Lord were meant to display His absolute, exclusive authority over the demonic realm. He was able to respond to each specific instance as the situation warranted because He was the Son of God, Who needed no special patterns or formulas to overcome His demonic foes.

This gives the believer today great comfort, for our Lord is in complete mastery over the forces of darkness. He can still exercise His sovereign authority to deliver and protect from demonic invasion. Yet in casting out demons, Jesus was *not* giving lessons in exorcism; He was demonstrating clearly Who He was. His deliverances were always simple, straightforward and immediately successful. Modern so-called deliverance ministries are at best a mere shadow of these mighty miracles. People today certainly do *not* cast out demons as Jesus did.

Finally, the demonic expulsions that Jesus accomplished were shown to be clearly regarded as miracles and are put alongside such other spectacular feats as instantly healing the sick and even controlling the forces of nature. Accordingly, the claim to cast out demons as Jesus did would imply a similar claim to be able to perform other miracles as well. If one could truly cast out demons just as Jesus did, it would be logical to assume that he could perform other miracles as Jesus did. One cannot separate the ability to cast out demons from the ability to perform miracles in general. We can have no "pick-and-choose" miracle ministries.

SUMMARY

We must reject denials that Jesus cast out demons during His earthly ministry. If Jesus did not cast out demons as the Bible says He did, one is left only with the dismal choices of saying Jesus deliberately lied, He did not know any better or the Gospel records simply cannot be trusted.

Jesus' demon expulsions contrasted sharply with the methods of His contemporaries. They used elaborate incantations, adjurations and religious ceremonies. While Jesus' methods varied, His word was prominent and powerful in casting out demons. His approach was always simple and dignified, and this style caused great astonishment among the witnesses of these events.

The demon expulsions of Jesus were significant in three ways. First, they were miracles, specifically miracles of healing. They fit the criteria of miracles, they were recognized as such by the populace, and they have a similarity of pattern and terminology with other miracles that Jesus performed. Second, they were kingdom-related signs, pointing to the authority and power of the King. They also authenticated the message of the gospel of the kingdom, and demonstrated that Satan's kingdom was being forcibly plundered, the way being prepared for Messiah's kingdom to begin. This occurrence caused violent clashes between Jesus and Satan's forces, which were graphically demonstrated when Jesus forced the demons to leave their victims. This demonstration also may explain the unusual outbreak of demon possession in Jesus' day, and the great number of expulsions that Jesus performed. Third, the words of the demons themselves underscored Jesus' identity as Messiah and Son of God and showed His absolute authority over the demonic realm.

CHAPTER THREE
THE APOSTLES: IN THE MASTER'S FOOTSTEPS

I n the minds of many believers today, the term "apostle" has the idea of "super Christian." Because of their great spirituality, it is claimed, the apostles were able to heal the sick, raise the dead and cast out demons. It is further believed that if others have the same depth of faith, they also can do these things. While it is true that the apostles were men of great faith, it is also true that their office was unique and foundational to the Church (Eph. 2:20; Rev. 21:14). A proper understanding of that office and its authority helps to put their ministry of casting out demons into proper perspective.

WHAT WAS AN APOSTLE?

It is quite common to hear many well-meaning Christians use the words "apostle" and "disciple" as if they mean the same thing. But, in fact, these words have different meanings. The apostles were twelve men who had the great privilege of occupying a special office. Jesus appointed them to an exclusive fraternity, with a closed membership and unprecedented powers. In order to better appreciate this exceptional office it is profitable to look at what the word "apostle" signifies.

The Meaning of the Word

The word "apostle" is a transliteration of the Greek word *apostolos*, which in turn is related to the verb *apostellō*. The basic meaning of *apostellō* is "to send forth."[1] Correspondingly, an "apostle" (*apostolos*) could be defined as "a messenger, one sent on a mission"[2] or also a "delegate, envoy, ambassador."[3]

A proper understanding of *apostolos* is greatly helped by an understanding of its Hebrew equivalent, *šālîaḥ*. While *šālîaḥ* does not appear in the Old Testament, its verb form, *šālaḥ* appears often. Among the rabbis, *šālîaḥ* had the fundamental meaning of one who was commissioned by the sender with the authorization to act in his behalf.[4] The rabbis described the idea clearly in their own proverb: "the one sent by a man (*šālîaḥ*) is as the man himself."[5]

In general usage, *šālîaḥ* was employed in both legal and religious circles. Legally, the *šālîaḥ* was commissioned or authorized by the one he represented to conduct such things as financial transactions. The *šālîaḥ* could, for example, make a financial pledge in the name of his sender. One could even become betrothed in marriage through a *šālîaḥ*, who legally performed all the ceremonies in the bridegroom's place.[6]

All of this reinforces and helps to clarify the use of the word "apostle" in the New Testament. In all of its 79 fully attested occurrences in the New Testament, "apostle" always pictures a man who is sent with the full authority of the sender.[7] In a general sense, "apostle" could refer to specially commissioned messengers of local churches (2 Cor. 8:23; Phil. 2:25), or, in broader terms, to any authorized representative (John 16:13). In most instances, however, the word is used of apostles of Jesus Christ, including the Twelve (Matt. 10:2; Rev. 21:14) and Paul (as in 1 Cor. 1:1, 2 Cor. 1:1; Gal. 1:1, 2; Eph. 1:1; Col. 1:1).

How They Qualified

When the meaning of the word "apostle" is understood and the New Testament is examined, four qualifications of apostleship can be seen. First, an apostle of Jesus Christ had to be chosen for that office immediately and directly by Christ Himself. The gospel records bear this out. In Luke 6:13, the twelve disciples were called apostles after they were chosen by Christ. In this case, the apostles were so called due to their commissioning as official representatives of Jesus.[8] He *chose* them. The same is true of the apostle Paul. He called himself an apostle "by Jesus Christ," indicating that Christ chose him directly as His authorized representative.[9]

Second, an apostle acted as a unique, authorized representative of Jesus Christ. An apostle was, in a sense, a "proxy" for Jesus. In Matthew 10:1 and 2 the twelve disciples are called apostles following their being given *authority* to act as His representatives. Jesus Himself confirmed this authority when He said, "He that receiveth you receiveth me" (Matt. 10:40). Because the Twelve were Jesus' personally authorized representatives, to reject them was to invite a judgment worse than that of Sodom and Gomorrah (Matt. 10:14, 15). The extent and nature of this authority can also be seen in Paul's statement of 1 Corinthians 14:37 where he stated, "If any man think himself to be a prophet, or spiritual, let him acknowledge that the things that I write unto you are the commandments of the Lord." Paul's commands can be regarded as the Lord's commands because Paul was Jesus' authorized representative, who was given authority to speak in Christ's name.

Third, an apostle had to be an eyewitness of the risen Christ. When Peter suggested that a replacement should be chosen to take the place of Judas Iscariot (Acts 1:15–26), he stated that the one chosen must ". . . be ordained to be a witness with us of his resurrection" (v. 22). When Paul defended his apostleship to the Corinthians, he said, "Am I not an apostle? . . . have I not seen Jesus Christ our Lord?" (1 Cor. 9:1).

Fourth, an apostle had to perform appropriate miracles that showed the apostle's claims to be true (see in detail below). When these qualifications are considered, we can safely conclude that the apostolic office was unique, and that the only ones who held it were the Twelve and Paul. Being Jesus' unique representatives and primary witnesses of the Resurrection, the apostles were foundational to the Church Age (Eph. 2:20). *There are not now—and there will never be—any others who can truly claim the title "Apostle of Jesus Christ"!*

MIRACLES: GOD'S "SEALS OF APPROVAL"

Why did the apostles perform miracles? Some today believe that miracles were intended to serve as a general aid to faith; therefore, these things should continue today to impress unbelievers and bring them to the Lord.[10] The New Testament, however, teaches that God gave the apostles the ability to perform miracles in order to confirm their message and to authenticate them as Jesus' genuine representatives and messengers. Miracles were in effect God's "seals of approval" upon the apostles' office and message. Three lines of proof support this contention.

First, Paul called signs, wonders and mighty deeds "the signs of an apostle" (2 Cor. 12:12). The word for "sign" here (sēmeion) meant "the sign or distinguishing mark by which something is known," then a "sign consisting of a wonder or miracle, an event that is contrary to the usual course of nature."[11] Among the Greeks, the term "sign" was used of a turning pylon in chariot races, a monument to a dead person marking his resting place, the symptoms of an illness, the ensign on a ship or the signet on a ring.[12] In every case, the word had to do with an object or circumstance that makes possible a specific understanding or insight.[13]

In 2 Corinthians 12:12, Paul stated that miracles were distinguishing marks of apostleship and thus authenticated the messenger and message, showing the apostles to be indeed the special representatives of Jesus Christ. In the New Testament, no miracles ever occurred except at the hands of Jesus Himself or His apostles or those who were directly ministered to by an apostle. If these signs and wonders were identifying marks of apostleship, it is logical to assume that they must have been *uniquely* connected to the apostolic office only. This implies that Christians in general cannot perform miracles like the apostles did. If they could, the miracles that the apostles performed could hardly serve as "signs of an apostle." Their uniqueness would be gone!

Second, the performance of miracles was directly related to apostleship in the apostles' original commission. Matthew 10:1 and 2 state: "And when he had called unto him his twelve disciples, he gave them power against unclean spirits, to cast them out, and to heal all manner of sickness and all manner of disease.

Now the names of the twelve apostles are these. . . ." Clearly, the power to perform these miracles was a key element in the apostolic commission and office.

Third, Hebrews 2:3 and 4 firmly contend that apostolic signs were meant to confirm the apostolic message.

> How shall we escape, if we neglect so great salvation; which at the first began to be spoken by the Lord, and *was confirmed* unto us by them that heard him [i.e., by the apostles]; God also bearing them witness, *both* with signs *and* wonders, and with [various] miracles, and [distributions] of the Holy Ghost, according to his will.[14]

So, then, miracles were specifically meant to authenticate the message of the apostles, whose office and credentials were totally unique.

CASTING OUT DEMONS AS A SIGN OF APOSTLESHIP

The New Testament clearly links the casting out of demons with the signs of an apostle. Casting out demons was thus understood to be a special and miraculous act. This can be established from three standpoints. First, the language describing both is similar. Demonic expulsions done by the apostles are directly called signs (*sēmeion*) in Acts 5:12–16. (The healing of those vexed with unclean spirits in verse 16 constitutes one of the signs of verse 12.) In Acts 19:11 and 12, the departures of evil spirits from some in Ephesus at the hands of Paul are called "special miracles" (*dunameis*). The vocabulary here is clearly parallel to 2 Corinthians 12:12, where mighty deeds (*dunamesin*) and signs (*sēmeia*) are called the "signs of an apostle."

Second, the casting out of demons by the apostles is almost always grouped with other extraordinary signs. Observe the following passages that name demon expulsions by the apostles, and note the other signs linked with them:

(1) Matthew 10:1—with healing all manner of sickness and disease;

(2) Matthew 10:8—with healing the sick, cleansing lepers, raising the dead;

(3) Mark 6:13—with healing accompanied by anointing with oil;

(4) Mark 16:17, 18—with speaking in tongues, handling serpents, drinking poison without harm, healing the sick;

(5) Acts 5:12–16—with healing the sick in general, and in particular by one's shadow coming over them;

(6) Acts 19:11, 12—with healing, when the sick came into contact with the clothing of the apostle.

From the above, it is evident that the New Testament puts the apostolic casting out of demons on the same level with the most spectacular signs, including even the raising of the dead.

Third, as it has already been pointed out, the casting out of demons was distinctly linked with the apostles' commission itself (Matt. 10:1, 2, 8; cf. Mark 3:13–15). According to Mark 6:7 and 13, demonic expulsions were the single most dominant aspect of the first apostolic preaching tour.[15] The casting out of demons particularly authenticated the apostles' message of the gospel of the kingdom (Matt. 10:7, 8), for it was a clear demonstration that Satan's kingdom was being vanquished and God's kingdom was near at hand.

THE PROBLEM OF MARK 16

What Is the Problem?

It has been shown that the apostolic office was unique and that certain "signs of an apostle" authenticated the apostles' message. Casting out demons was shown to be one of those signs. Consequently, only apostles or those directly connected with the apostles could cast out demons or perform any other sign-miracles. Mark 16:17, however, states that some of these signs, including casting out demons, would follow "[those] who believe." What is the identity of those who believe? Charismatics and others who wish to argue for the present-day exercise of apostolic sign-gifts by any believer flatly state that "[those] who believe" includes any disciples who believe Jesus' statement and submit to His lordship.[16] If they are right, any believer can be expected to be able to cast out demons. If they are wrong, however, the passage argues once again for an apostolic limit for this ability.

A Debate about Words

One of the difficulties with using this passage to support *any* position is the fact that a great debate persists over whether the words of Mark 16:9–20 are genuine. The sheer number of endings to the book that are in existence demonstrates the problem.[17] The great Greek scholar A. T. Robertson has correctly stated concerning the manuscript evidence that "the facts are greatly complicated."[18] His conclusion provides good caution on this matter:

> The great doubt concerning the genuineness of these verses (fairly conclusive proof against them in my opinion) renders it unwise to take these verses as the foundation for doctrine or practice unless supported by other and genuine portions of the N. T.[19]

A Suggested Approach

The confusion over whether Mark 16:9–20 is authentic should cause wise Bible students to beware of basing *any* doctrinal position upon this passage alone. However, when understood correctly, Mark 16:9–20 does not contradict in any way the idea that casting out demons and other miracles were signs of apostleship. Several careful observations make this clear.

First, the subject of the entire passage is the eleven apostles (16:14), to whom the Lord appeared, confronting them for their unbelief. It is only the Eleven who are present when the commission of verse 15 is given; and only the Eleven are thus in view in verses 19 and 20, where the beginnings of their ministry are summarized.

Second, the purpose of these miracles is clearly stated in verse 20: "And they went forth, and preached every where, the Lord working with them, and *confirming* the word with signs following." The same word used here for the signs (*sēmeion*) is also used for the miracles of verses 17 and 18 (*sēmeia*, v. 17). The signs of these verses, then, must be interpreted as authenticating the apostles' word and applying to their ministry.

Third, "[those] who believe" should be connected with the apostles. The connection can be made in two ways. One way is to understand the reference to be to the belief of the apostles, who had just been upbraided for their unbelief. This would make the verse one of encouragement to the Eleven.[20] The other way is to see "[those] who believe" as identified with the believers of verse

16, who were saved directly through the apostles' preaching (v. 15).[21] Clearly those in view in verse 16 believe for salvation. The believers of verse 17 seem to be linked to those in verse 16 by the fact that in *both* verses, aorist participles are used to describe them (*ho pisteusas, ho apisteusas*, v. 16; *tois pisteusasin*, v. 17).[22] In either case, the apostles' ministry is ultimately in view.

Fourth, neither Acts nor the Epistles record anybody other than an apostle, or one who came in contact with an apostle, performing these signs. As the record relates to casting out demons, the only ones who were said to have done this are the apostles in general (Acts 5:12, 16), Paul in particular (Acts 16:16–18; 19:11, 12) and Philip the Evangelist (Acts 8:6, 7), upon whom the apostles had laid hands (Acts 6:5, 6).

To summarize, because of the textual problems, no doctrine should be based solely on Mark 16:9–20. When carefully considered, however, Mark 16:14–20 underscores the fact that casting out demons was an apostolic credential that authenticated the apostolic message and that only apostles or sometimes those who had *direct* contact with an apostle were authorized to cast out demons.

HOW THE APOSTLES DID IT

When one examines the Biblical data describing how the apostles cast out demons, he discovers that far less material is available for this than for Jesus' methods. Nevertheless, enough information is available to draw some conclusions.

A General Pattern

When examining the available New Testament information, one can mark the apostolic practice of casting out demons by three distinct traits.

First, the demonic expulsions performed by the apostles were *immediately* successful. As in the case of Jesus, the Bible records no long, protracted struggles or prayer meetings to deliver the demonized. When Paul cast the demon out of the girl with the Pythonic spirit, the demon came out "the same hour" in response to Paul's command (Acts 16:18). The spirit was commanded to leave and forthwith left. In Ephesus, evil spirits left their diseased victims when the sick came into contact with items of clothing from Paul (Acts 19:12). Obviously no protracted process occurred here. Furthermore, it is hard to imagine multitudes being freed from demons only after long struggles (Acts 5:16). The apostles would not have had the time to deal with so many people at once unless cures could be immediately brought about. Also, long laborious battles with demons would hardly have been unique signs of apostleship. As it has been pointed out earlier, incantations and long processes were the norm for Jewish and Greek exorcists in the New Testament era. As with the demon expulsions of Jesus, the immediate casting out of demons by the apostles was seen as unprecedented by the populace at large, showing apostolic authority and the uniqueness of their actions.

Second, the apostolic casting out of demons followed no set pattern as far as the method was concerned. Usually, the practice was done by a command in Jesus' name (Mark 16:17). This is directly stated in the account of Paul and the young lady of Philippi (Acts 16:18), and it seemed to be a general practice involved in the performance of other spectacular miracles as well (Acts 3:6; 4:10). The action of some Jewish exorcists in Ephesus, who attempted to cast out demons "by Jesus whom Paul preacheth" (Acts 19:13), may possibly suggest that they had heard Paul casting out demons in Jesus' name.[23]

This was not, however, a pattern that never varied. At times demons were cast out without even the physical presence of the apostle or *any* command in Jesus' name. This is exactly what happened in Ephesus where it is stated:

> And God wrought special miracles by the hands of Paul: so that from his body were brought unto the sick handkerchiefs or aprons, and the diseases departed from them, and the evil spirits went out of them (Acts 19:11, 12).

This passage presents the picture that demonized people (who manifested the usual terrible physical symptoms) were coming into contact with some pieces of material that Paul had used as sweat rags and aprons while engaged in his trade of leather working. These were brought forth, and mere contact with them resulted in deliverance from evil spirits. This was an unusual method indeed!

A similarly unusual "method" of casting out demons may possibly be indicated in Acts 5:15 and 16. The latter verse states that those vexed by evil spirits were *healed* by Peter, and the preceding verse pictures the sick being laid in the streets to be *healed* by Peter's shadow. If some of the "sick" in the streets were ill because of demonization (which was at times the case), they were delivered by Peter's shadow! From these examples, it is apparent that demons were cast out by the apostles in a variety of ways, with no single pattern always involved.

A close connection with the miracles of Jesus can be observed in the general pattern of demonic expulsions performed by the apostles. In their pre-Pentecostal ministry, the apostolic mission and miracles of casting out demons were described in similar terms as the ministry of Jesus. Jesus went about preaching the gospel of the kingdom, accompanied by the casting out of demons (Matt. 4:23–25; Mark 1:14, 15, 21–39). The apostles were commissioned to announce the same message (Matt. 10:7), to be accompanied by the same authenticating signs (Matt. 10:1, 8; Mark 3:14, 15; 6:12, 13; Luke 9:1, 2).

The demonic expulsions that the apostles performed after Pentecost had similarities to several of the miracles of Jesus. Take for example Paul's command to the demon inhabiting the girl in Philippi. His command, which resulted in its departure (Acts 16:18), is similar to the oft-repeated rebuking command of Jesus to demons (as in Mark 1:25; 9:25; Luke 9:42). In addition, the extraordinary deliverances from demonic illness that resulted from touching Paul's sweat rags and aprons is reminiscent of the healing of those who touched the fringe of Jesus' cloak (cf. Mark 5:27 ff.; 6:56).[24]

From an examination of the above, one can conclude that apostolic demon expulsions were astounding miracles. Every recorded instance (except one: Matt. 17:14–21; cf. Mark 9:14–29; Luke 9:37–43) shows complete success, and the success was immediate. While commanding the demons in Jesus' name may have been the "norm" for demonic expulsions, spectacular success was also achieved at times through merely coming into contact with an apostle's garment. The casting out of demons by the apostles was often strongly reminiscent of some of Jesus' miracles.

All of this clearly shows that the practice of casting out demons by the apostles authenticated them as Jesus' official representatives and their message as from God. Their expulsions of demons were "signs of an apostle." Certainly nobody today is casting out demons as the apostles did.

Lessons from a Failure

The single seeming exception to all of this success is found in Mark 9:14–29 (cf. Matt. 17:14–21; Luke 9:37–43). In this instance, a man whose son was demonized (Mark 9:17) with resultant violent epileptic seizures (Matt. 17:15) came to Jesus for help. He had previously brought the boy to the apostles, but they could not cure him (Matt. 17:16); they could not cast the demon out (Luke 9:40). This record is the only instance in the New Testament where the apostles failed to deliver a demon-possessed person who was brought to them for deliverance. Jesus gave three reasons for their failure: (1) because of the demon itself ("this kind," Mark 9:29); (2) because the demon would come out only by "prayer and fasting"; and (3) because of the apostles' lack of faith.

A superficial reading of the passage (Mark 9:14–29) has caused some to see here a protracted struggle with the demon, involving an extended prayer session accompanied by fasting and an extra measure of faith. The apostles' failure and Jesus' instruction is then applied to present-day exorcism as well.[25] Thus some people give lack of faith as a reason why some present-day exorcisms end in failure, or at best partial success.[26] To evaluate this issue properly, one must examine four areas—the concepts of fasting, prayer, faith and the application of this passage to the present time.

It is the idea of fasting that most strongly gives the passage the idea of a protracted battle. Fasting requires a considerable period of time! However, the term "and fasting" should not be regarded as a part of the original text for several reasons: (1) Textual criticism renders it doubtful. While most manuscripts contain "and fasting," the authorities that omit it are important.[27] (2) Jesus had clearly approved of His disciples' refusal to fast as long as He was with them.[28] (3) The textual tradition of several other passages (Matt. 17:21; Acts 10:30; 1 Cor. 7:5) indicates a strong tendency for early copyists of Scripture to add the words "and fasting" to the original text.[29] (4) The circumstances rendered a sufficient time for fasting here impossible.[30] The boy was brought to the apostles for immediate help; and when it was not forthcoming, the father went directly to Jesus.

Once it is realized that fasting was not involved in this incident, one no longer has any reason to insist that the prayer mentioned here took a long time. It could have lasted a few hours or a few seconds. The latter is far more likely and does not conflict with an idea of quick demon expulsions by the apostles. At least one other reference gives a New Testament example of "quick" prayer before the performance of an apostolic miracle. In the raising of Dorcas, Peter kneeled and prayed just before commanding her to arise (Acts 9:40). Apparently the apostles resorted to prayer before they could perform some particularly difficult miracles.

Assuredly, lack of faith was involved in the apostles' failure. But what did this mean? Faith involves in its most basic sense a positive response to what God has revealed. It could thus be said that their faith in Jesus as the Messiah had not failed; but rather they had not had faith in their commission to cast out demons.[31] Lenski summarized:

> When the evil spirit in the boy defied the nine disciples, instead of allowing themselves to be defeated their faith should have risen up in its might, should have appealed to Jesus in a fervent prayer that he make good his promise to them to expel demons. They would thus have won the contest, the demon would have disappeared. The disciples did not think of prayer, they let their faith droop at once and thus failed. The prayer need not be audible, a fervent sigh in the heart would be enough.[32]

All of the comments made in connection with this incident were made to the apostles (here called "disciples," Mark 9:18, 19, 28, 29). They were not made to believers of all ages. A summary of the passage suggests the following scenario: The apostles had come against a particularly strong, evil demon ("this kind," Mark 9:29), and the demon resisted their command. Instead of affirming by prayer their faith in Jesus' commission to them to cast out the demon, they gave up in discouragement. Jesus was not setting down a formula of fasting and protracted prayer meetings for all believers as a means of casting out demons. He had in mind simple trusting prayer connected with faith before the apostles performed an especially difficult sign-miracle. Thus this passage does not conflict with the teaching that the apostles could immediately deliver the demon possessed.

When It All Came to an End

The early New Testament era clearly assumed the reality of demonism. When, however, one considers the prominence of demon possessions and expulsions in the Gospels, Acts by contrast shows great reserve. The number of demon expulsions recorded is not as large as one might expect in a period when belief in possession by evil spirits prevailed.[33] The old cliché about a "demon behind every bush" was accepted as a reality in the culture in which the apostles lived. Yet the New Testament seems to reject this belief firmly.

The last recorded demon expulsions took place in Ephesus (Acts 19:11, 12), around A.D. 53–56.[34] Shortly thereafter, around A.D. 68,[35] the Gospel of Mark was written. At this time, Mark stated that authenticating signs, including demonic expulsions (Mark 16:17), had already ceased (Mark 16:20). The leading verb in Mark 16:20 is "preached" (*ekēruxan*), an aorist tense indicating a past act. The terms "working with" (*sunergountos*) and "confirming" (*bebaiountos*) are present participles. According to Greek syntax, these participles do not represent time after this preaching, but time contemporary with it.[36] Thus when the writer wrote, he knew that apostolic preaching confirmed by signs (of which demonic expulsion was one) was already past, and he referred to it as such.

If this theory is correct, it should be confirmed by New Testament indications that other signs had ceased as well. This is, in fact, exactly what one finds when he examines Biblical data. Smith wrote:

> The last miracles recorded in the New Testament took place about A.D. 58 (Acts 28:3–9). Around A.D. 60 Paul's "brother, and companion in labour, and fellow-soldier," Epaphroditus, while

visiting Paul became sick "nigh unto death"; but he was not healed miraculously (Phil. 2:25–30). About A.D. 62 Paul's own "true child in the faith" (1 Tim. 1:2) apparently had a stomach ailment which remained uncured (1 Tim. 5:23). Around A.D. 64 one of Paul's associates was so seriously ill that Paul had to leave him behind, uncured (2 Tim. 4:20). Yet earlier, Paul had been instrumental even in restoring life to the dead![37]

The testimony of the book of Hebrews further confirms this. Hebrews was written prior to A.D. 70, probably in the 60s.[38] In Hebrews 2:3 and 4 the writer asked:

> How shall we escape, if we neglect so great salvation; which at the first began to be spoken by the Lord, and was confirmed unto us by them that heard him; God also bearing them witness, both with signs and wonders, and with [diverse] miracles, and gifts of the Holy Ghost, according to his own will?

In this passage, the same grammatical pattern can be found as in Mark 16:20. The leading verb "was confirmed" is aorist (*ebebaiothē*), and "bearing witness" (*sunepimarturountos*) is a present participle, again referring to action that took place at the time of the main verb. This serves to verify Mark's similar statement. Clearly, the apostolic practice of casting out demons ceased before A.D. 70.

SUMMARY

The apostles officially represented Jesus Christ in a unique sense. They were given His authority, and they spoke for Him. To authenticate their position and message, they displayed certain signs or miracles, known as "signs of an apostle." One of these signs consisted of the casting out of demons. Being only one of many signs of an apostle, demon expulsions cannot be separated from such other signs as healing the sick, raising the dead, speaking in tongues and supernatural protection. Even though serious textual debate remains over the authenticity of Mark 16:9–20, the passage actually confirms other New Testament teaching that casting out demons was an apostolic sign. "[Those] who believe" in Mark 16:17 are either the apostles or those directly ministered to by the apostles. In any case, the demon expulsions are called "signs" that "confirmed" the apostolic message (Mark 16:20).

The apostolic practice of demon expulsions was characterized by (1) immediate success; (2) no set patterns; and (3) striking parallels to some of Jesus' miracles. The failure of Mark 9:14–29 provides no contradiction to this statement; but it shows that in particularly difficult circumstances, a brief prayer accompanied by faith in the commission given by Christ was necessary for success. Since the casting out of demons was an apostolic sign-miracle, the practice ceased with the death of the apostles. Various New Testament references pinpoint the date to sometime between A.D. 56 and 68.

CHAPTER FOUR
OTHERS WHO CAST OUT DEMONS

I t has been demonstrated that the casting out of demons was a sign-miracle. In the ministry of Christ, the many demon expulsions authenticated the message that "the kingdom of heaven is at hand." They also pointed to Jesus as the Son of David who would reign as King. The casting out of demons likewise authenticated the message of the apostles, who were the unique representatives of Jesus.

In the light of this, one might suppose that only Jesus and the apostles were able to cast out demons. This is not the case, however, for others performed the same miracles, although some others failed. How does this fact relate to the concept of understanding demonic expulsions as signs of an apostle? The answer to this question is found by looking at who these people were and exactly what they did.

THE SEVENTY

Apparently the Seventy were successful in casting out demons during their ministry (Luke 10:1–20), much as the apostles were. When the Seventy returned to Jesus at the close of their mission, they said, "Lord, even the devils [demons] are subject unto us through thy name" (Luke 10:17). Previously, Jesus had ". . . appointed other seventy also, and sent them two and [by] two before his face into every city and place, whither [where] he himself would come" (Luke 10:1). Their ministry was aimed specifically at preparing the way for the Messiah in the villages that He would go to prior to Calvary.[1] It involved a moral (and spiritual) preparation, challenging the nation to open the gates to its rightful King and to accept His rule.[2]

In order to authenticate their message, Jesus gave the Seventy power and authority similar to that of the Twelve, in effect making them "temporary apostles." Five lines of proof establish this statement. First, while the Seventy are not specifically called "apostles," the verbal form *apostellō* is used of their commission by Jesus in Luke 10:1. (He "sent them forth," *apesteilen*.) Second, they were to preach the same message that Jesus and the apostles had preached—that the kingdom of God was at hand[3] (Luke 10:9, 11; cf. Matt. 4:17; 10:7). Third, both the Seventy and the Twelve were given the ability to perform miracles to authenticate their message (Luke 10:9; cf. Matt 10:1, 7, 8). Specifically, the Seventy were given the power to "heal the sick," and inasmuch as demonic expulsions were to be regarded as a kind of healing miracle, the authority to cast out demons must have been included here. Fourth, the same judgment would await those who rejected the Seventy as those who rejected the Twelve (Luke 10:10–12; cf. Matt. 10:14, 15). Fifth, the same general instructions were given to the Seventy and the Twelve (Luke 10:3–12; cf. Matt. 10:9–16). They were both sent as lambs among wolves; neither was allowed to take provisions for the way; both were to pronounce peace upon homes where they were welcomed; both were to shake off the dust of their feet as a testimony against cities that rejected them. From the above comparisons, we come to this inescapable conclusion— the Seventy, for at least this mission, were regarded as Jesus' apostles.

But did the Seventy retain the power to cast out demons after this mission? Was their apostleship temporary or permanent? A careful examination of the evidence suggests that the apostleship of the Seventy was only temporary. Perhaps the best proof of this fact can be found in the commission of the Seventy. Their activity was geographically limited to the cities that Jesus would visit prior to His death (Luke 10:1). This fact clearly implies that their ministry was meant to fill a temporary need.[4] By way of contrast, the commission of the Twelve was less geographically limited (Matt 10:5, 6), and they were the selected companions of Christ on a longer basis.[5]

Furthermore, Christ did not recommission the Seventy after the Resurrection. But the contrary is true for the Twelve. In John 20:21 Jesus said, "As my Father hath sent me, even so send I you." The Great Commission was given to the Eleven (Matt. 28:16–20), and their preaching was to continue being confirmed through sign-miracles (Mark 16:15–20). From this truth it is plain that Jesus directed Himself primarily to the Eleven during the days between His resurrection and ascension—preparing them to continue as His authoritative representatives through whom He would lay the foundation of His Church.[6] Throughout all of this time, no mention is made of the Seventy. In fact, after their brief mission of Luke 10 was completed, the Seventy disappear completely from the pages of Scripture as a group.

Thus we have no indication that the Seventy permanently retained their power to perform healings (including casting out demons).[7] Their ability to cast out demons during this one mission strongly supports the contention that casting out demons was a sign of apostolic authentication and was not practiced by all believers in general.

THE JEWISH EXORCISTS

The Sons of the Pharisees

Matthew 12:27 mentions that certain persons that Jesus called "your [sons]" allegedly cast out demons. The context of this statement was one of the seemingly constant attacks upon Jesus by the Pharisees. Jesus had just cast a demon out of a blind and dumb man, and as a result the people began to question whether Jesus could be the Son of David (Matt. 12:22, 23). The Pharisees then charged that Jesus cast out demons by the power of Beelzebub (v. 24). In part of his reply, Jesus said:

> And if Satan cast out Satan, he is divided against himself; how
> shall then his kingdom stand? And if I by Beelzebub cast out

[demons], by whom do your children [sons] cast them out? therefore they shall be your judges (Matt. 12:26–27).

What is the identity of "your sons"? The best answer to that question is that they were disciples of the Pharisees. Jesus was addressing the Pharisees directly, and in direct address, the genitive "*your* sons" (*hoi huioi humōn*) refers to the object of the address, namely the Pharisees.[8] For Jesus to speak to the Pharisees, referring to "your sons," and mean His own or any other disciples, is grammatically impossible.[9]

The term "sons" (*huioi*) can have several meanings. The meaning that makes the best sense here, however, is "of a pupil, follower, or one who is otherwise a spiritual son."[10] These sons are not, therefore, the physical sons of the Pharisees, but are instead their own followers who were experts, of whom they approved and were proud, because they were able to cast out demons.[11]

Controversy exists over whether and how these Pharisaic adherents cast these demons out. Only two basic positions can be taken in this controversy: either they did or did not cast out demons. Among those who say that the Pharisaic sons did not cast out demons, Jesus' statement that they did cast them out is usually called an *argumentum ad hominem*. This simply means that in His argument Jesus was meeting the Pharisees on their own terms and not expressing a personal judgment concerning whether or not they actually had cast out demons.[12]

This idea is possible but highly debatable. It seems logical to suppose that some positive results were achieved by these exorcists. What other reason would explain the Pharisees' belief that their colleagues were successful? Furthermore, the Lord's argument would have lost its meaning if the Jews were unable at least to appear to cast demons out. On the contrary, Jesus' entire argument presupposes some apparent success in the Pharisees' exorcisms.[13]

Among those who believe that these Jews actually *did* perform exorcisms, opinions are once again divided. Some say that Jesus' question logically demanded the admission that these Jews really did successfully exorcise demons and that it was done in the power of God—through fasting, prayer and sincere faith on the exorcists' part.[14] The problem with this view is that rabbinic exorcisms in the days of Jesus did *not* consist of simply pious prayers to Jehovah, perhaps accompanied by fasting. Rabbinic exorcisms of Jesus' day involved revolting and disgusting extremes, consisting of many baseless superstitions, mostly the outcome of a mixture with heathen elements. Edersheim correctly observed, "Greater contrast could scarcely be conceived than between what we read in the New Testament and the views and practices mentioned in Rabbinic writings. . . ."[15] Thus if these exorcists actually did cast out demons by God's power, God is seen as authenticating and validating their superstitious practices.

It is best to assume that the Pharisees' colleagues did actually bring about a deliverance at times from demon possession for some people. The demons did leave—but not under compulsion. The demons permitted themselves to be exorcised by these exorcists,[16] possibly to further the false notions then believed concerning demonism and to further the spread of false Pharisaic teachings. One might object to this interpretation by saying that it contradicts Jesus' statement about Satan casting out Satan. On close scrutiny, however, no contradiction takes place. Jesus referred only to the hostile invasion of Satan's kingdom by the power of God, in which Satan suffers real and permanent loss. Jesus did not refer to Satan's methods that are designed to deceive and extend his kingdom. Obviously Satan has the power to assign his demonic forces where he sees fit or to remove them from a particular place, if only temporarily (Matt. 12:43–45), in order to confuse or to deceive. When demons leave in this manner, no division in Satan's kingdom takes place, nor is Satan casting out Satan. Rather, Satan is acting with keen strategy to *further* his kingdom.[17]

Thus, this passage does not teach that pious believers in general can or did cast out demons against their will. Instead it provides a sober warning against judging the validity of so-called exorcisms based simply upon experiences or observations. Demons may voluntarily leave their victims to promote false doctrines, false ministries and false ideas concerning the nature of demon expulsions. The exorcisms of the Pharisees' colleagues in no way parallel the demonic expulsions of Jesus and His apostles. Jesus used them in His argument against the Pharisees to show their inconsistency. They lauded the exorcisms of their colleagues, but rejected One Whose results were far more spectacular and were performed in the power of the Spirit of God.

The Sons of Sceva

The sons of Sceva are called "exorcists" in Acts 19:13, the only place in the New Testament that uses this term. These men are noteworthy for their failure to cast out demons by using the name of Jesus. During Paul's ministry in Ephesus, he apparently cast out a number of demons in the name of Jesus. Seeing this, the sons of Sceva attempted to expel a demon by saying, "We adjure you by Jesus whom Paul preacheth" (Acts 19:13). The result was not only that the demon did not leave, but also the demonized man gave them a beating (Acts 19:15, 16). Three questions must be answered in order to understand this passage properly.

First, who were these men? They were called the "sons of Sceva, a Jew, and chief of the priests" (19:14). No Jewish high priest named Sceva is known outside of this verse. The title could have been used here in the broad sense to refer to the head of a priestly family (as in 5:24);[18] or the title "Jewish chief priest" could have been Sceva's own lying description of himself.[19] As to their activities, they were traveling Jewish exorcists. The use of the term "exorcist" (*exorkiston*) suggests that they attempted to cast out demons by using formulas, charms and incantations. This idea is also suggested by the fact that, among those who practiced magic in ancient times, Jews enjoyed high respect because it was thought that they had particularly effective spells at their command.[20]

Second, did they really cast out demons? It is possible that their entire practice was a sham.[21] There is no problem, however, in acknowledging that at times they did bring about a cure for the victims of demonization—but it was a cure that the *demons* brought about by leaving their victims voluntarily. This is similar to the situation of "your sons" in Matthew 12:27.

Third, why did they fail in this instance? The answer to this question is found in the demon's reply to the exorcists: "Jesus I know, and Paul I know; but who are ye?" (Acts 19:15). Many scholars feel that these exorcists failed because of unbelief.[22] It is unquestionably true that these men were unbelievers; but that is not what the demon pointed to as the cause of their failure. He said to them literally, "But you, who are you?" The word "you" (*humeis*) places the emphasis upon the *identity* of the exorcists, not their faith. The demon knew the identity of Jesus; He was the sovereign Lord Whose authority extended even over Satan's realm. He also knew the identity of Paul, who was Jesus' representative and, therefore, had been given the signs of an apostle, including the authority to cast out demons. But these exorcists' authority was self-proclaimed; therefore, the demon refused their command, lest Jesus' name get any further glory. This episode thus harmonizes well with the concept that demon expulsions were miracles of apostolic authentication.

SOME AT THE JUDGMENT

At the Judgment some people will use their alleged exorcism of demons as proof of their fitness to enter the kingdom (Matt. 7:21–23). Jesus said:

> Many will say to me in that day, Lord, Lord, have we not prophesied in thy name? and in thy name have cast out devils [demons]? and in thy name done many wonderful works? And then will I profess unto them, I never knew you: depart from me, ye that work iniquity.

It is noteworthy that these persons (1) claim to have cast out demons; (2) claim to have done it in Jesus' name; and (3) claim to have done other mighty works (*dunameis*) as well. However, these are workers of iniquity. The present tense of this participle (*ergazomenoi*) suggests that, in spite of their protests to the contrary, their lives are characterized by disobedience and lawlessness. This fact demonstrates clearly that a relationship never existed between themselves and Jesus—He never knew them.[23]

Did these unbelievers actually cast out demons? The form of the negative "not" (*ou*) used in their statement suggests that they expected a positive answer (i.e., "*Surely* we have cast out demons . . .").[24] It is highly unlikely that simply because these people used the name of Jesus, He actually did enable them to cast out demons despite their lost condition. The failure of the sons of Sceva under similar circumstances would argue against this supposition. Only two other possibilities exist: (1) They really did not cast out demons but only thought that they did; or (2) the demons left voluntarily as may have been the case with the sons of Sceva and the sons of the Pharisees.

In either case, the passage gives a solemn warning. The fact that people make claims to cast out demons or even to perform other miracles in Jesus' name does not mean that the miracles are of God. The exorcisms may appear to be real but in reality may not be done with Jesus' authority. Deuteronomy 13:1–3 clearly states that it is not apparent miracles but the Word of God that decides what is from God and what is not.

AN ANONYMOUS DISCIPLE

In Mark 9:38–40 the apostles saw one who was casting out demons in Jesus' name. Because he was not of the Twelve, they rebuked him. John said to Jesus, "Master, we saw one casting out [demons] in thy name, and he followeth not us: and we [forbade] him, because he followeth not us" (v. 38).

It is doubtful that this individual was an exorcist like the sons of Sceva, who simply saw Jesus' name as a magical formula, without any commitment to Jesus Himself.[25] Jesus stated that the man was "for us" (v. 40) and could not lightly speak evil of Him (v. 39). He may have been someone who had heard Jesus preach and believed in Him but who had not as yet developed any close relationships with Jesus' followers.[26]

This passage gives scant information regarding the man's method or his success, and opinions are divided as to who he was and exactly what he did. Some assert that the man actually did perform a miracle in the power of Christ, and that this demonstrates the fact that a non-apostle could perform miracles.[27] The text is not so clear, however.

Apparently, as John and the other apostles were traveling through Galilee, they met a man who was using Jesus' name to cast out demons. The term "casting out" (*ekballonta*) is a present participle, indicating that this action was in progress. Whether the man was successfully casting out demons or just attempting to do so when the apostles came by is uncertain. It is clear, however, that the apostles spent some effort trying to stop the man, as seen in the imperfect form of the verb "forbid" (*ekoluomen*), which also suggests that the man refused to stop.[28]

Jesus' words to the apostles reflect concern for both the man and their attitudes, and cannot be used conclusively to determine what the man actually did. They had just been debating who among them was the greatest (Mark 9:33–37). Instead of having personal concern for the man and patience regarding the development of his faith, the apostles displayed jealousy over a man who had "invaded their territory." Instead of steadfastly forbidding him, they should have recognized that his action displayed a positive attitude toward Christ (v. 39). The man was not against them but for them (v. 40).

In summary, Christ used the occasion to rebuke His apostles for their wrong attitude toward the man. He does not comment on the validity of the exorcism but uses the episode as a "teaching tool" to lead the Twelve to a right attitude toward their apostleship and toward others. Therefore, the episode should not be used as a clear endorsement of the nonapostolic practice of casting out demons.

PHILIP THE EVANGELIST

Philip the Evangelist unquestionably was able to cast out demons, and he was highly successful in doing so. In describing the ministry of Philip, Luke wrote:

> Then Philip went down to the city of Samaria, and preached Christ unto them. And the people with one accord gave heed unto those things which Philip spake, hearing and seeing the miracles which he did. For unclean spirits, crying with loud voice, came out of many that were possessed with them: and many taken with palsies, and that were lame, were healed (Acts 8:5–7).

This passage shows that Philip was able not only to cast out demons but to perform other spectacular miracles as well. How is it that Philip was able to do these things? Did he simply have greater faith than others? Or is there some other answer?

A careful examination of Scripture indicates that Philip's supernatural ability was directly related to his contact with the apostles. It can be traced back to Act 6:6, where the apostles laid hands upon Philip and his six associates. The laying on of the apostles' hands meant more than the fact that the Seven were being set apart for a special blessing; it made them in a limited sense apostolic associates who shared in their work.[29] Accordingly, these associates were able to manifest the "signs of an apostle," authenticating the apostolic message to their hearers. Three lines of proof demonstrate this fact.

First, until this time, nobody other than an apostle worked miracles. After hands were laid upon the Seven, however, both Stephen (Acts 6:8) and Philip were able to perform miracles and signs.

Second, while Philip was able to perform miracles, including casting out demons, no unusual proofs of divine activity were conferred upon his converts, *until an apostle's hands were laid upon them.*[30] In Acts 8, the apostles Peter and John came to Samaria from Jerusalem, prayed for Philip's converts and laid their hands upon them. As Peter and John were laying their hands upon these people, the people manifested unusual signs of the Spirit's presence (Acts 8:14–17), which established the authority of the apostles among the Samaritans.[31] This incident is so crucial to a proper understanding of the apostolic authority to confer gifts and abilities upon others through the laying on of hands that B. B. Warfield called it "the cardinal instance."[32]

Third, other New Testament passages demonstrate the apostolic ability to confer spiritual gifts or abilities upon others through the laying on of hands. In 2 Timothy 1:6 Paul exhorted Timothy to stir up the gift of God, "which is in thee by the putting on of my hands." The word "by" (*dia*) is also used in an identical sense in Acts 8:18, where Simon saw that *through* (*dia*) the laying on of the apostles' hands the Spirit was manifested. When used with the genitive case, *dia* in these instances can have the meaning of agency.[33] Thus the hands of the apostle Paul were the agency through which Timothy received the gift at this commissioning.

The same truth is evident in Romans 1:11, where Paul longed to see the Roman believers, "that I may impart unto you some spiritual gift, to the end ye may be established." While some question remains concerning how the church at Rome was founded, evidently the church had never benefited from the direct, personal ministry of an apostle.[34] Paul thus desired to impart to them attesting sign-gifts personally; and in the light of the previously cited passages, it seems likely that he planned to do this through the laying on of hands.[35]

From these passages, one can conclude that Philip's ability to cast out demons was a miraculous gift conferred upon him when the apostles laid hands upon him. It attested the apostolic message. This is apparent in Acts 8:6, which states that the people heeded Philip's *message*, "hearing and seeing the miracles which he did." It is striking that this is the *only case* after Pentecost that directly states that someone other than an apostle cast out demons; and it was done in connection with the apostles. Clearly, Philip's ministry provides a strong argument *against* the claim that casting out demons can be performed by consecrated believers of any age.

SUMMARY

While the apostles and Jesus were not the only ones who cast out demons, a careful survey of other real and alleged instances of demonic expulsions in the New Testament tends to reinforce the idea that the casting out of demons was an authenticating sign-gift that was peculiar to the Gospels and apostolic period. In several alleged instances of successful exorcism, the demons may have left of their own accord to advance false doctrine, erroneous ideas concerning demons and counterfeit ministries. The colleagues of the Pharisees (Matt. 12:27), the sons of Sceva (Acts 19:13, 14) and those at the Judgment (Matt. 7:21–23) may fall into this category. The man that the apostles forbade (Mark 9:38–40) is somewhat of a mystery. Not enough information is available to determine exactly what he did and whether he had actually cast demons out or was only attempting to do so. The Bible gives only two clearly attested instances where someone other than Jesus or the Twelve cast out demons—the instances of the ministry of the Seventy and Philip. The Seventy were in effect "temporary apostles," and Philip received the ability after the apostles laid hands upon him. All of these facts reinforce the idea that the chief reason for casting out demons was to authenticate the message of Christ and the apostles.

CHAPTER FIVE

EXORCISM AND THE PRESENT

I n spite of the fact that the New Testament clearly presents the ability to cast out demons as a miraculous apostolic sign-gift, many persons today claim the contrary. People from a broad theological spectrum within professing Christianity practice exorcism. Some claim that the New Testament establishes a gift of "Biblical exorcism." Many point to present-day experiences of deliverance from demon possession as proof that "Biblical" exorcisms are still valid. Do the Epistles shed some light on believers' abilities in this area? Do they teach a gift of "Biblical exorcism" being given to certain believers today? Does the Bible give "tests" to help determine whether or not a person is truly possessed? And how do we interpret present-day experiences? The purpose of this chapter is to provide some answers to these legitimate questions, especially in the light of the teaching of the Epistles.

IS THERE A GIFT OF BIBLICAL EXORCISM?

One of the most striking facts concerning the casting out of demons is that the Epistles make not a single reference to it. They give no examples, no instructions and no passages that specifically refer to the casting out of demons as a gift. Demonic expulsions may possibly be included in references to some other more general gifts, however.

A Connection with the Gift of Healing

First Corinthians 12:9 refers to "gifts of healings" (*iamatōn*). This particular word "healing" (*iama*) is used in the New Testament only in this chapter (12:9, 28, 30), but the verbal form "to heal" (*iaomai*) is used twenty-eight times in the New Testament. While *iaomai* is used figuratively for the healing that comes through forgiveness of sins,[1] the vast majority of its uses in the New Testament are connected with physical healing (twenty-two times—all in the Gospels and Acts). It is in this latter sense that the term is obviously used in 1 Corinthians 12:9, and thus gifts of healing refer to restoring health to the body.[2] It should be made clear that this ability to heal is here called a gift, which should be kept distinct from enjoying healing as an answer to prayer. Healing as an answer to prayer is a privilege that is open to all believers; such healing may happen instantly, gradually or not at all. But the gifts of healing involved a miraculous ability, given to only a few in the Apostolic Age.[3]

The verb "to heal" is also used in the Gospels and Acts in connection with the casting out of demons in the ministry of Jesus and the apostles. It is used directly to describe the result of casting out demons (Matt. 15:28; Luke 9:42; Acts 10:38), and in at least one case is employed in a passage where physical healings and demonic expulsions are *both* referred to (Luke 6:17–19). The use of this word is logical to describe deliverance from demon possession, since the most obvious and serious result of the demonized state in the Gospels was physical malady. This verb may thus provide a logical link between demonic expulsions and gifts of healings, showing that an aspect of those gifts may have included the ability to cast out demons.

Another possibility regarding demon expulsions is to relate them to the gifts of "powers" (literally "workings of powers," *dunameōn*[4]) found in 1 Corinthians 12:10. The general meaning of *dunamis* is "power, might, strength; ability, power to perform," and *dunamis* is therefore used of the power of performing miracles.[5] It refs to the general power of working miracles other than healing the sick, as possibly illustrated by the apostles in the deaths of Ananias and Sapphira, the raising of Dorcas and the smiting of Elymas with blindness.[6]

The phrase "works of powers" may also contain a reference to demonic expulsions.[7] Two lines of proof suggest this. First, the word "power" (*dunamis*) is used in connection with Jesus' encounters with Satan. Jesus defeated Satan and cast out demons by means of His power (*dunamis*; Luke 4:36).[8] Second, in the commission of the Twelve, power (*dunamis*) was given to them to enable them to cast out demons (Luke 9:1).[9] Third, Paul's demonic expulsions at Ephesus are called "special miracles"; literally, "powers" (*dunameis*).

On the other hand, while the exact phrase "works of powers" is used in several places of the miracles of Jesus (Matt. 14:2; Mark 6:14), it is never used of casting out demons. Because of these problems, it may be best to see the casting out of demons as an aspect of the gifts of healings.

What This Means for Today

It has been shown that demonic expulsions were often classified in the New Testament as a kind of healing. Similar words were used for other healings and casting out demons. Also similar methods were used with both, and similar reactions came from those who witnessed these miracles. These facts, as well as the verb "to heal" (*iaomai*), clearly link demonic expulsions with other forms of healings, and all might be classified under "gifts of healings."

Because of this, it is neither logical nor consistent with the New Testament pattern to separate the ability to cast out demons from the ability to heal miraculously the sick in general. Jesus, the Seventy (Luke 10:9, 17), the Eleven (Matt. 10:1; Acts 5:12, 16), Philip (Acts 8:6, 7) and Paul (Acts 19:11, 12) were *all* able to heal the diseased *and* cast out demons. One cannot say with Biblical support that demonic expulsions are "exceptional miracles" that are valid for today, while other miraculous healings are not.[10] If the "gift of exorcism" is claimed for today, then other healings involved in "gifts of healing" should also still be regarded as valid and should be practiced by the same individuals.

It has already been established that casting out demons was a "sign of an apostle" (2 Cor. 12:12). This point has been demonstrated by an examination of the terms used, the grouping of demonic expulsions with other extraordinary signs and the fact that casting out demons was inseparably linked to the apostolic commission. Exactly the same arguments can be used to show that other healings were signs of an apostle. The same words are used in both cases. Apostolic signs and healings are called "signs" (sēmeion; Acts 5:12; 15, 16) and "miracles" (dunameis; Acts 19:11, 12). Healings are connected with handling serpents and drinking poison without harm (Mark 16:17, 18), raising the dead (Matt. 10:8) and deliverance through one's shadow (Acts 5:12–16) or clothing (Acts 19:11, 12). The apostolic commission and healings are also vitally connected (Matt. 10:1; Mark 16:17, 18).

It can be stated, then, that gifts of healings—including casting out demons—are sign-gifts, which were given by the Spirit for the purpose of authenticating the apostles and their message. Since they were signs of an apostle, gifts of healings had to be confined to the apostolic era; otherwise they could not have been uniquely apostolic signs. Since apostolic signs, including the casting out of demons, were shown to have ceased by A.D. 68, present-day "casting out of demons" must be another kind of phenomenon.

Apart from their unique authenticating of the message of Christ and the apostles, gifts of healings in general, and in particular the casting out of demons, had limited value. Jesus Himself warned of the danger of casting demons out of a man who refused to trust Christ: ". . . The last state of that man is worse than the first" (Matt. 12:45). The great priority even in the apostolic era was to preach the gospel. This was to be the ministry of the apostles (and of all), and demonic expulsions were to be a confirmatory sign, but without question subservient to the preaching of God's Word. At no time in the New Testament era did an individual have the ministry of casting out demons, with the gospel taking a position in the background.

New Testament miracles of healing in general, and demonic expulsions in particular, were consistently able to bring about immediate cures.[11] It is as inconsistent to think of one who is demonized being delivered over hours, days or weeks as it is to think of a lame person being healed over a similarly lengthy period of time. Those with the gift of healing *never* had such experiences, yet such experiences are common today. Present-day exorcisms may take hours, days or even weeks.[12] There is no Biblical parallel to the many present-day experiences that often involve long-term deliverances. While some of these experiences may indeed be real, they simply are not an evidence of the gifts of healings. They do not fit the Biblical definition or pattern of that gift.

HOW CAN WE RECOGNIZE DEMON POSSESSION?

It is obvious that before one can cast out demons, he must be sure that the problem confronting him is indeed one of demonization. This sounds simple enough; but it will be found to be no small problem when one surveys the literature of those who are personally involved in counseling the demonized.

Ensign and Howe, for example, state that irrational or compulsive behavior that is immoral or hurts the testimony and integrity of the believer is almost always an evidence of demonic activity in the believer's life. They list a number of problems that may fall into this category, such as fear, rage, pride, anger, mental confusion, sexual sins, temper, lying, gluttony, depression, feelings of resentment and even sickness or infirmity.[13] As one looks at these symptoms, he is struck by the number of so-called symptoms of demonic activity that could easily have other explanations as well. A review of Galatians 5:19–21 is helpful at this point. Paul stated:

> The acts of the sinful nature are obvious: sexual immorality, impurity and debauchery; idolatry and witchcraft; hatred, discord, jealousy, fits of rage, selfish ambition, dissensions, factions and envy; drunkenness, orgies, and the like (NIV).

In other words, an individual can be involved in extreme activities such as compulsive sexual immorality (orgies), fits of rage and even witchcraft—and these activities can be prompted simply by the individual's sinful nature, without any demonic source at all! How can one detect the difference, then, between normal sins of the flesh and similar symptoms of demonic invasion?

In addition to this, there is the widespread belief that demons can hide in their victims. Dickason states, "Some cases may be more unnoticed and perhaps even unknown by the person demonized."[14] It is also asserted that demons may attempt to disguise their presence by deliberately mimicking various physical and mental disorders that could stem from more "normal" causes.[15] It is therefore practically impossible to determine clearly most so-called demon possessions from symptoms alone.

The only avenue open to determining real demon possession in these cases is therefore assumed to be a supernatural enabling of some sort. That supernatural enabling is commonly seen as either a special intuitive ability to detect the presence of demons or a special confrontational test that will cause them to manifest themselves. Proponents of these practices usually claim Scriptural support in connection with the Biblical gift of "discerning of spirits" (1 Cor. 12:10) or a Biblical injunction to "test the spirits" (1 John 4:1–4).

A Gift of Discernment

First Corinthians 12:10 speaks of a gift of "discerning of spirits." The term "discern" (*diakriseis*) means "distinguishing, differentiation of good and evil."[16] This much seems clear. But what does discerning of spirits relate to?

Some interpreters see this as a reference to demonic spirits and conclude that this gift is closely related to exorcism[17] because it enables one to determine whether or not a person is energized by a demon.[18] This means that one with the gift of "discerning of spirits" can know in difficult situations whether a person is really demonized, and deal with him accordingly. Rodger Bufford shows how this gift would function at the counseling level:

> Perhaps the best diagnostic strategy for counselors is to combine behavioral observations with intuition or spiritual discernment. In seeking to reach a conclusion about the nature of a particular person's problems, the helper would look for converging evidence from these two sources of information. When both point toward probable demonic influence, reasonable confidence can be placed in that conclusion. Similarly, where neither of those provides affirmative indications, demonic in-

fluence can be ruled out with some confidence.

This approach is consistent with that proposed by Michael Green. He recommends discernment, and the spiritual gift called "discernment of the spirits" as very helpful in recognizing whether a person is demonized. On one occasion, for example, upon entering a room in which a possessed person was standing, he noted, "I felt an immediate, almost palpable sense of evil. . . ." In addition, Green advocates diagnosis by means of a careful case history to discover whether important indicators are present.[19]

This interpretation has three problems, however. First, the New Testament accounts show no real problem in determining whether or not a person was demon possessed. Even the unregenerate at times were able to discern properly the difference between illness caused by demonism as opposed to disease (Mark 7:24–30; Matt. 17:14–21; cf. Mark 9:14–29). Second, even if this gift were directly related to casting out demons, we have no reason to assert that it was a permanent gift. If the gift were related to casting out demons, it could have been directly connected with an apostolic sign-gift and thus be temporary in nature.[20] Furthermore, it is placed in the text between two temporary gifts—the gifts of prophecy and tongues.[21] Third, the gift of discerning spirits can be clearly established as relating to gifts of prophecy.

This connection to gifts of prophecy can be seen when one understands the "spirits" of 1 Corinthians 12:10 as being connected with the "spirits of the prophets" mentioned in 1 Corinthians 14:32. This connection is clearly illustrated by the context of 1 Corinthians 12:10. Here one can find a sort of couplet: discerning of spirits is seen as a complementary gift to prophecy, just as interpretation is complementary to speaking in tongues.[22]

How did the gift of discerning of spirits relate to prophecy? It has usually been suggested that it involved the ability to identify the source of "revelations" given by the prophets in the assembly. Through this gift people were enabled to determine whether a prophet was speaking from God, the impulses of his own mind or at the dictation of Satan.[23] So by exercising this gift, one could ultimately know whether the revelation given by the prophet was true or false.[24]

The actual use of this gift is alluded to in 1 Corinthians 14:29, "Let the prophets speak two or three, and let the others judge." The word "judge" here (*diakrinetōsan*) is the verbal form of the word "discern" (*diakriseis*). Apparently the other prophets were primarily involved in the exercise of discerning of spirits. From this passage comes the suggestion that discerning of spirits involved the application of prophecy to the congregation. Luther suggested that these other prophets who "discern spirits" would judge and see to it that the prophesying was rightly done.[25] Whatever the exact function of the gift of discerning of spirits may have been, it was clearly connected with prophecy and had nothing to do with casting out demons. Furthermore, since prophecy itself was a temporary gift, it can be safely assumed that the genuine gift of discerning of spirits is no longer being given today.[26]

Testing the Spirits

Much attention has been given to 1 John 4:1–3, which many claim has reference to demons. It states:

> Beloved, believe not every spirit, but [test] the spirits whether they are of God: because many false prophets are gone out into the world. [By this] know ye the Spirit of God: Every spirit that confesseth that Jesus Christ is come in the flesh is of God: And every spirit that confesseth not that Jesus Christ is come in the flesh is not of God: and this is that spirit of antichrist, [of which] ye have heard that it should come; and even now already is it in the world.

Some identify the spirits of 1 John 4:1 with demons or evil spirits.[27] They claim that these verses speak of a sort of confrontational test that can be used to determine demon possession. This test might in one form involve asking the demon if Jesus Christ has come in the flesh.[28] If a person is truly indwelt by a demon, it is asserted that the demon will deny that Jesus Christ has come in the flesh.[29] Three lines of support are given in favor of this theory: (1) elsewhere the New Testament calls demons "unclean *spirits*" (Mark 1:23, 26), or "spirits" (Rev. 16:13, 14); (2) this passage further explains how the gift of "discerning of spirits" (1 Cor. 12:10) could be exercised, that gift being understood as a test of demon possession; (3) experience validates this theory—in short, it works.

This theory presents several real problems, however, that cause one to question its validity. One of these problems centers around the usage of the word "spirit." Although the New Testament sometimes refers to demons as spirits, the term has a much broader usage, and the context is often an important key to its meaning. Neither the immediate context of 1 John 4:1–3 nor the entire context of 1 John contains a single reference to demons. Furthermore, when the word "spirit" is used elsewhere in the New Testament of demons, it normally is linked with a definitive adjective, such as "an *unclean* spirit" (Mark 1:23). Also, it has been conclusively shown that the discerning of spirits has nothing to do with casting out demons.

In addition, a difficulty is encountered in the very nature of this test, if indeed it is claimed to be a test for demon possession. Nowhere else in the New Testament can one find a single example of either Christ or anyone else using a test to determine demonization.[30] The phenomenon of demonization was extreme and obvious. A further problem is seen when one closely examines the meaning of "test" (*dokimazete*). The word has the idea of "to test, try, prove in the hope and expectation that the test will prove successful."[31] If the test here were one for demonization, one would be testing with the hope of finding the victim genuinely demonized!

Next, a serious problem exists in connection with the historical context of 1 John. There is no question that this book was at least partly polemical in nature. John was not writing to warn of demon possession; he was writing to warn against a prevailing heresy. The heresy involved was a form of pre-Gnosticism, which did not accept the concept of Christ's coming in the flesh.[32]

Finally, not even empirical evidence supports this theory. Adherents claim that a demon *always* denies that Christ has come in the flesh; but this experience is not as uniform as some wish it would be. Some who practice the casting out of demons frankly admit they have heard demons say that Christ has come in the flesh.[33] Biblical accounts also describe experiences where demons have confessed Christ (Luke 8:28). In the light of these problems, the idea of using 1 John 4:1–3 as a test for demon possession must be rejected.

Crucial to a proper understanding of this passage is the meaning of the term "spirit" (*pneuma*). The term can at times be defined as "a frame of mind, disposition, influence."[34] This definition of "spirit" fits well with the meaning of this entire passage.

In 1 John 3:24, the reference is to the attitude or disposition that a believer displays in his life. John states that a believer knows Christ abides in him by the attitude or disposition that He has given him. That attitude displays itself in obeying Christ's commands (3:22) and loving the brethren (3:23).

The thought of attitude or disposition is carried into 1 John 4. The believer is not to accept any erroneous doctrinal attitude or disposition toward Christ that a so-called prophet displays. He should put his doctrinal attitude toward Christ to the test with the hope that he passes the test and is correct in his attitude. The reason why John recommended that believers check the attitude of these so-called prophets concerning the doctrine of the Incarnation was because of the historical problem of pre-Gnostic teachings creeping into the church. The attitudes of these men concerning the Incarnation and Gnostic doctrines could be easily uncovered by facing them with the confession of verse 2. If the men confessed Christ as having come in the flesh, then believers could know that their attitude in this area was of God. If they denied this doctrine, they displayed an attitude that was similar to the doctrine of antichrist, which was already in the world.

It can thus be recognized that the teaching of this passage has nothing to do with checking for demonization. Nor does it have any reference to demons in any other sense. John is warning believers against being gullible to false prophets whose doctrine is heretical.[35]

WHAT ABOUT PRESENT-DAY EXPERIENCES?

Because of the great emphasis upon experiences in much of the literature dealing with casting out demons, we need to examine experience as it relates to both doctrine and facts.

WHAT DO EXPERIENCES PROVE?

The use of experience as proof and endorsement of present-day exorcism practices is widespread. Otherwise-sound evangelicals who stand squarely upon Scripture as the sole authority for their faith and practice have sometimes caved in to "experiences" in the area of the demonic. It is rare indeed to find a recent book dealing with demonology that is not liberally sprinkled with a generous amount of "experience" accounts. Sound Biblical exegesis is often modified or discarded in favor of experience as a basis for correct doctrine. Regarding the relationship between doctrine and experience, Merrill F. Unger commented as follows:

> Of course, doctrine must always have precedence over experience. Nor can experience ever furnish a basis for biblical interpretation. Yet, if consistent experiences clash with an interpretation, the only inference possible is that there is something wrong with either the experience itself or the interpretation of the Scripture which runs counter to it. Certainly the inspired Word of God never contradicts valid experience. The sincere truth-seeker must be prepared to revamp his interpretation to bring it into conformity with facts as they are.[36]

It is the last sentence of this statement that deserves careful attention. Who or what determines "the facts as they are"? Is it a certain quality or quantity of experiences that determine what makes something a fact? Or which authorities can be trusted to be unquestionably true? The "facts as they are" certainly do not support the Virgin Birth. Should one discard this doctrine because human experience today always argues against it? Jesus said, "Sanctify them through thy truth: thy word is truth" (John 17:17). Truth and absolutes can be found in the Word of God. When that truth is modified or cast aside in favor of experiences, no matter how abundant they may be, the door has been opened for a theological relativism that will give birth to chaos.

A further complication that arises when one tries to interpret supposed incidents of demon possession and deliverance is related to the moral nature of demons and Satan. If Satan is pictured as anything in Scripture, he is pictured as a deceiver.[37] Jesus said that no truth is in him, he is the father of lies, and lying is his native language (John 8:44). Paul warned that he can masquerade as an angel of light to further his trickery (2 Cor. 11:14) and that Eve was deceived by his cunning (2 Cor. 11:33). John further declared that Satan deceives the whole world (Rev. 12:9; 20:10). The demonic forces that Satan commands partake of the same nature. The Bible calls them lying spirits (1 Kings 22:22; 2 Chron. 18:21, 22), and one of their specialties is spreading false teaching (1 Tim 4:1). Demons clearly have an agenda of deception.

Furthermore, the spirit world cannot be seen. Paul warned that the believer's foe is not flesh and blood, but an incorporeal, invisible enemy that he calls "spiritual forces of evil in the heavenly realms" (Eph. 6:12, NIV). We cannot see what Satan and his forces are planning, nor are we privy to his strategy sessions. Given their deceptive nature, we can expect that demons can manipulate experiences and skew the "facts" in order to promote confusion and further their own agenda. This causes all interpretations of demonic experiences to be suspect unless they are measured against the Word of God. Measuring experiences by the Word is absolutely essential because the Word of God gives the only completely trustworthy and authoritative information about these wicked unseen foes. This includes many exorcism experiences. The words of Albert Runge are most appropriate here. He stated:

> I have become convinced that many exorcisms are power play setups by the demons themselves. They choose an exorcist who may lack wisdom, the knowledge or the authority to challenge them effectively. They choose the timing as well as the audience. The whole process is under their control from the beginning to the end.[38]

This warning also applies to talking with demons. The Bible warns forcefully against attempts to contact or extract information from the spirit world. Deuteronomy 18:9–22 is particularly applicable here.[39] Verses 9–12 condemn intercourse with the world of evil spirits, while verses 14–22 give the reason,[40] which is that the believer is to rely only on information that God has provided through His prophets—not information provided by the spirit world. The example of Jesus' conversation with a demon in the episode with the Gadarene demoniac (Mark 5:1–20) cannot be used as a justification for talking to demons either. Jesus' ministry has already been shown to be unique; and, in addition, this conversation was contrary to Jesus' normal practice of *not permitting demons to speak* (Luke 4:41). Also, how could one ever give credence to statements made by beings whose very nature is to be deceptive? There is no way apart from the Word of God to know if even sincere believers are not being manipulated by demons or being fed false information.

How Experiences Can Be Explained

In the realm of demonization, one must be extremely careful not to misinterpret experiences. Present-day "exorcisms" can be explained in four ways. First, problems may be falsely attributed to demon possession when, in fact, the source of such problems may be found elsewhere. The most common mistakes relating to false identification usually involve the failure to recognize mental derangement or the fallen nature of man. Certain kinds of mental disorders, for example, may manifest themselves in bizarre or violent behavior, terrible fears or hallucinations; yet the problem may be unrelated to demonism.[41] Here are some Biblical examples of gross moral sin or bizarre behavior not due to demon possession: Lot's incest with his own daughters (Gen. 19:30–38); homosexuality and the rape of a woman by the Benjamites (Judg. 19); the dismemberment of a concubine's body by her husband (Judg. 19:29, 30); and the murder of seventy half-brothers by Abimelech (Judg. 9:1–5). These were terrible and even bizarre acts, but they apparently were the result of man's wicked sinful nature, not demon possession. Human depravity is terrible indeed, but it must not be confused with demonization.

Second, demons themselves may mislead by deliberately and voluntarily leaving their victims, thus creating a false impression of being cast out. Cases in point are the exorcists of Matthew 12:27 and other exorcists such as the sons of Sceva. There is no way apart from Scripture to determine if a demon's departure is faked or if he really is compelled to leave. Demons may voluntarily depart to further their own purposes or to promote false recognition in association with *any* ministry.[42]

Third, many so-called Biblical exorcisms may in fact be more correctly understood to be prayers for *divine* compulsion to remove these evil spirits from their victims. Many protracted prayer-battles fall into this category. These experiences, which are sometimes valid, are incorrectly called "Biblical exorcisms," when in fact they bear little resemblance to the demonic expulsions performed by Jesus and the apostles. We have no reason to believe that Jesus cannot sovereignly cast demons out even today, when earnest believers call upon Him to deliver the hapless victims of demonization. This is not, however, a display of casting out demons as it was in the New Testament. It is a different phenomenon.

Fourth, some present-day exorcisms may be explained by the power of suggestion. It is interesting to observe that certain types of "demon possession" sometimes seem to follow exorcists who warn about the dangers of these kinds of possessions.[43] A sincere Christian counselor who works with the demonic mentioned in passing that most of his counselees had already suspected a demonic source to their problems when they came to him.[44] This suggests a possible subliminal conditioning to finding a demonic source to problems among at least some counselees.

A Dangerous Diversion

Not only are present-day exorcism experiences misunderstood easily, but they can also be dangerous. One of the dangers involves avoiding responsibility for sinful behavior.[45] Immoral behavior, for example, can wrongly be ascribed to a "demon of lust" instead of the willful decision to walk in the flesh and sin against God. In such cases, personal accountability is denied by projecting the moral aspect of the individual's behavior on to an alleged demon.[46] If no demon is present, the immoral behavior may resume because the individual does not take responsibility for his sin.

Another danger of majoring on demon experiences and exorcisms can be found in looking for obvious manifestations of demonism, while ignoring other Satanic forms of influence that are far more subtle. Some believers may come to regard demon possession as a primary manifestation of the forces of evil. In reality, Satan could actually encourage interest in demon possession in hopes that believers will become careless about other less conspicuous forms of influence by the powers of evil.[47]

The failure to get qualified help for people who truly need it may be a further danger of majoring on demon experiences. Instead of getting possible needed medical help or help from a qualified counselor, one can jump to wrong conclusions concerning demonization—and in so doing greatly harm the one who has the problem.

Yet another problem can result from majoring on demon experiences—the acceptance of unbiblical ministries. It has already been shown that the departure of demons from the "demonized" is in itself no proof that they have been cast out by the power of God. For example, in Ceylon, the Sinhalese peasants have a popular ritual called the *Sanniyakuma*. It is designed to appease and cast out the *Sanni-yakku*, demons of ill health. All of this is done in Buddha's name.[48] Individuals from a wide range of doctrinally diverse backgrounds have claimed to cast out demons in the name of Jesus.[49] Are all of these religious and doctrinal positions valid because their experiences are positive and beneficial? The preoccupation with experiences can lead one to an acceptance of false doctrine because it is "proved" to be correct by experience. If one accepts the validity of exorcism based upon experiences, he has logically opened the door to accept any false doctrine upon the same basis. This is perhaps the most dangerous result of majoring on modern-day accounts of exorcism.

A SUFFICIENT BIBLE

It has been repeatedly pointed out that the subjective and often misleading experiences reported with the demonic need an objective standard with which they can properly be evaluated— and that standard is the Word of God. Few, if any, in the conservative, evangelical movement have historically challenged that statement. Yet, in practice some are beginning to take a different position. Some of those involved in ministries of casting out demons are superficial and careless in their understanding of Scripture. Others, however, are normally thorough and careful students of the Word of God. They are honest, sincere believers who have a deep concern for helping the hapless victims of occultic and demonic involvement. Yet, unfortunately, much of their understanding and methodology in this area is based upon sources of information other than the Bible. This is a key issue in the whole discussion of dealing with the demonic. Is the Bible *alone* sufficient to guide us in our understanding of demonism and demon possession? Or do we also need information gleaned from such sources as clinical case studies and the experiences of others to equip us for this aspect of ministry? That question can be answered only when one carefully looks at what the Bible asserts its role to be in equipping people to live a life pleasing to God.

What the Bible Claims for Itself

The greatest passage dealing with the nature and function of the Word of God is undoubtedly 2 Timothy 3:16 and 17. Paul wrote:

> All scripture is given by inspiration of God, and is profitable for doctrine, for reproof, for correction, for instruction in righteousness: That the man of God may be perfect, [thoroughly] furnished unto all good works.

Note that Paul was dealing with a body of literature called the Scriptures. While the immediate context here is the Old Testament, the term has a wider meaning. When Paul wrote these words, the term referred to a body of sacred literature that included more than the Old Testament;[50] it included many apostolic writings as well. Peter used the same word of Paul's writings (2 Pet. 3:16). Accordingly, the word "Scripture" here can be applied to the New Testament as well.[51]

The great theological truth states that the Scriptures are inspired. The word used here is *theopneustos*, from *theos* ("God") and *pneō* ("to breathe"). It might better be translated, then, as "God-breathed" or "God-spired."[52] Probably no Greek term could have made a stronger assertion that the Bible is the direct, creative product of God.[53] The "breath" of God often symbolized God's all-powerful creative work (Gen. 2:7; Ps. 33:6); hence the Bible is claimed to be unique, the direct result of God's creative activity.

Great theological truths such as this are, however, often stated in passing, when the writer had some other goal in mind. So it is here, for the main point of Paul's statement involves the use of Scripture. Because of what the Scripture is (a God-breathed book), it is therefore useful as a practical tool for instruction in living. Its instruction involves teaching in general, reproof, correction and discipline in righteousness.[54] This provides a framework for the whole process of counseling, including the resources and methodology to be used.[55]

Yet even the use of Scripture has a goal—to render the believer ". . . perfect, [thoroughly] furnished unto all good works." The words "perfect" and "[thoroughly] furnished" come from the same Greek root word. The noun form "perfect" is the Greek word *artios*, which carries the idea of completeness or being properly fitted.[56] The verbal form "thoroughly furnished" is *exertismenos*. It is a compound of *artios*, "to fit" and *ex*, "out";[57] hence meaning "to fit someone or something out or equip him." It was used of a ship being properly supplied with oars or of "an oil press in working order and *completely furnished*" (italics mine).[58] So the Scripture claims to be able to bring the believer to a suitable state for Christian moral action,[59] and to supply all of the instruction necessary for a believer to live a life pleasing to God.

Now the Bible does not claim to give all the answers in areas such as medicine, biology or history (even though it is accurate in what it says in these areas). However, it *does* claim that God has given us "all things that pertain unto life and godliness" (2 Pet. 1:3). Therefore when it comes to having a relationship with God, what the Christian life is all about, how we are to live it and the power for doing so, the Bible claims to be both *authoritative* and *complete* in its instruction.[60] Jay Adams has summarized the point well:

> Paul says, then, that there is no counseling situation for which the man of God is not adequately equipped by the Scriptures. All of the answers that he and his counselee need for pursuing the four comprehensive activities mentioned above are in the Bible. There is no need for eclecticism. This passage very plainly says that *all* that we need as the basic foundation and framework for helping others and helping ourselves has been given to us.

You, Christian counselor, have the resources. The resources are not in the outside expert, the resources are not in the
counselee, nor are they in ourselves; the resources are in God.
All of the resources are in God. That is the Bible's answer and,
therefore, that must be the Christian's viewpoint. The God of all
resources graciously has given them to us fully in His Word.[61]

Are We Left without Instruction?

It has been stated earlier that the Bible gives no direct instruction concerning how to recognize demon possession or cast
out demons. The Gospels and Acts contain only some historical
examples of Jesus, the apostles and a few selected others casting out
demons. The Epistles are entirely silent on the subject. This
silence presents a serious problem for those who advocate various
forms of modern deliverance ministries. Rodger Bufford, for one,
recognizes this problem. He openly questions whether the Gospel
accounts are adequate in dealing with various forms of demonic
influence, and suggests six limitations that the Gospels have in
this area.[62] He warns, "Thus, we should be cautious about conclud-
ing that all instances of demonic influence will exhibit the
symptoms most often associated with demon possession in the
Gospels."[63] In other words, for Bufford, the Scriptures are plainly
insufficient in and of themselves when we attempt to counsel the
demonic.

C. Fred Dickason has for years counseled believers who have
suspected problems with demons in their lives. He claims to have
encountered at least 400 *genuine believers* who were actually in-
habited by demons.[64] Dickason is representative of those who
would forcefully defend the sufficiency of Scripture but would also
claim that the Scriptures provide only *a framework* for how to
recognize and deal with demon possession.[65] This means that in
areas where the Bible does not give sufficient evidence (such as the
demon possession of a believer[66]), it is both proper and logical to
look for other lines of proof. Dickason writes:

First, we must answer that nothing can stand on the same
level of authority as the Bible, the revealed Word of God
inerrant in the originals and a sufficient guide to doctrine and

practice. Experience is not equal in authority when it comes to determining absolute truth. However, just as science has found the truth of God's world in its research, so may genuinely evaluated and reliably documented experience find truth in this matter. It is not a case of elevating experience to the same level as the Bible. We have previously treated this stand in detail.[67]

In observing the above statement, one comes to the conclusion that, according to this line of reasoning, the Bible is both sufficient and insufficient. A Biblical base for casting out demons is claimed, but much is borrowed from experience, clinical considerations and even secular psychology. So while claiming the sufficiency of Scripture, such ministries must actually go outside the Scriptures and turn to human opinions and experiences with demons for answers.

A further attempt to justify the use of non-Biblical experiences as a help for dealing with the demonized comes from an analogy that is suggested between believers who are demonized and believers who have cancer. The argument proceeds as follows: The Bible gives us parameters of information concerning what a believer is, as well as the fact that believers can be diseased. But it does not give us specifics concerning whether a believer can have cancer. That is determined through investigation and clinical or scientific evidence. And when we evaluate evidence, we can determine that Christians can indeed get cancer. If clinical evidence can be legitimately used to show that Christians can get cancer, why can't similar kinds of evidence be accepted to show that believers can be demonized?[68]

The problem with this analogy is that it is not, strictly speaking, an analogy at all. Cancer is an amoral problem. However, according to the symptoms described by modern counselors of the demonic, demon possession is certainly *not* an amoral problem. We are told that demon possession can be associated with perverted sexual thoughts,[69] sin associated with the old nature,[70] homosexual tendencies[71] or even unrestrained anger and rage that destroy a family.[72] These are not amoral issues!

The Bible never claims to be a book of diagnosing disease, but it *does* claim to be a book of diagnosing moral and spiritual problems. In fact, it claims that equipping the believer for every good work is its *exclusive* domain, and that it is fully sufficient for instruction in these areas. The silence of Scripture in such matters as diagnosing and treating demon possession speaks forcefully to the fact that those practices *must not be an essential issue.*

Critics of this viewpoint have repeatedly called this a "weak argument from silence."[73] An argument from silence it truly is; but given the claims that Scripture makes for itself, such an argument can hardly be called "weak." This is a silence that roars!

"Experiences with the demonic" are said to infer that a dear young Christian woman who spent time daily reading and memorizing the Word could not live a victorious Christian life until she was delivered from seven demons that had secretly bound her;[74] that not even being saved can at times free a person who has been demon-possessed since childhood due to his ancestors' occultic involvement;[75] and that such moral problems as all-consuming sexual desires and masturbation can be resolved in some believers' lives only through discovering and casting out hidden demons.[76] In cases such as these, repentant faith, trusting Christ as Savior, the new birth and daily meditation on and memorization of Scripture are inferred to be insufficient; these unfortunate Christians will supposedly remain bound in sin or never have their problems successfully resolved until they can find an "expert" who has insight into how to test for the presence of hidden demons and somehow cast them out.

Since the Bible gives no such tests or instructions, we are apparently left to rely on experiences and so-called clinical evidence as the means to victorious Christian living in these areas. The practical implication is that the Bible is insufficient for equipping individuals such as these for godly living; and that the Church is therefore inadequately prepared for every good work. It is asserted that *many believers* are suffering from unknown demonic invasion—a state that is seriously hindering their walk with God and devastating their lives. Yet the Bible is *completely silent* in how to deal adequately with these supposed cases. Could a truly sufficient Bible virtually ignore matters that are supposedly so vital to successful Christian living and still be sufficient? The answer to that question must be a resounding no.

SUMMARY

When the New Testament is closely examined, no specific gift of "Biblical exorcism" can be found. Because of its close association with healing miracles, it is probable that the "gift" of casting out demons was an aspect of the general gift of healings, which was one of the "signs of an apostle." As signs of an apostle, gifts of healings ceased by the close of the Apostolic Age. Present-day experiences of deliverance from demons are thus different in nature from the New Testament phenomenon.

The association that is often made between casting out demons and the gift of discerning of spirits (1 Cor. 12:10), as well as testing the spirits (1 John 4:1–4), is an invalid one. These passages, when examined closely in their context, have nothing whatever to do with demon possession. In fact, there is *no* direct teaching *anywhere* in the New Testament concerning how to determine demon possession. The Bible gives only historical examples.

Modern experiences of casting out demons cannot be used to prove any doctrinal position because of the possibility that demons can "fake" exorcism through voluntary departures from their victims and because of the deceptive nature of demons themselves. Several other explanations for modern exorcisms exist. Some so-called Biblical exorcisms may in fact be better understood as prayers for divine compulsion to remove the demons from their victims. While these experiences are sometimes valid, they are not the same as the New Testament phenomenon of casting out demons.

Finally, looking to experiences and case studies to develop a methodology for counseling the demonic at least implies that Scripture alone is insufficient to instruct and equip us for godly living. Since passages such as 2 Timothy 3:16 and 17 and 2 Peter 1:3 clearly claim otherwise, we must reject such a counseling methodology.

CHAPTER SIX
DEALING WITH THE DEVIL

I t has been shown that the Bible gives no tests that can be used to determine demon possession. It has also been shown that the Epistles are significantly silent with regard to the whole issue of demon possession. The Bible gives no instructions concerning how to deal with it. One might conclude from this fact that the Epistles contain no instruction regarding how to deal with demonic attack in general. This is not the case, however, for the Epistles do contain warnings about how to deal with the Devil and his wicked cohorts.

THE GREAT BATTLE AND THE PROVISION OF GOD

The epistle to the Ephesians might be called the "Epistle of the Church." In it the apostle Paul sets forth the Church in all of its greatness: its existence due to the sovereign will and calling of God (chap. 1), its formation through salvation by grace (chap. 2) and its unique position in the program of God (chap. 3). Since the church is ". . . his body, the fulness of him that filleth all in all" (Eph. 1:23), it is not surprising that the Enemy would engage in vicious and prolonged conflict with it. Believers are thus a target—the target of an invisible, powerful and genuine Enemy, whose army is dedicated to their destruction. With this reality in view, Paul ends his epistle of the glory of the Church by giving intensive instruction concerning its Enemy—his nature and his plan and what to do about it. Ephesians 6:10–20 thus forms the most extensive discussion of the provision of God for victory to be found anywhere in the New Testament. Since every believer must face the power of Satan and his demonic hordes, he must have a full working knowledge of this passage.

The Battle Plan

In the opening verses of this key passage (v. 10, 11), Paul gives believers God's battle plan against the Enemy. This plan involves three key points. The first is that the believer must go in the strength of the Lord. Paul wrote, "Finally, my brethren, be strong in the Lord, and in the power of his might" (6:10). The command to "be strong" (*endunousthe*) is a present passive imperative in the Greek. This means that the strength Paul has in mind comes from God (passive voice), is to be a regular part of the believer's life (present tense) and is absolutely essential if victory over Satan and his demons is to be realized (imperative mood).

Being in battle against Satan is not a game. The foe is too powerful to be defeated by believers who are ignorant of their position and provisions in Christ and who refuse to yield to God. Being made strong in the Lord involves conscious yieldedness to God and reliance upon His power for victory. No matter how great the past victories or how blessed the spiritual experiences they may have enjoyed, believers *must* realize that they are vulnerable to satanic or demonic shipwreck in their lives if they decide to cope in their own strength and refuse to walk in humble dependence upon God.

The second key ingredient to God's plan of victory is to "put on the whole armour of God" (6:11). Paul penned these words while in prison. And he saw many Roman soldiers during that time—possibly more than he cared to! It could be that a soldier, dressed in his military armor, was standing by even as Paul wrote. Observing the protection that the armor afforded the Roman soldier, Paul drew a parallel with the protection that God gives the believer, one who has enlisted in His service. The believer is to clearly appropriate God's provision (which will be discussed in greater detail later) if he is to achieve victory.

The third key ingredient to God's plan of victory involves strategy. The believer must depend upon God for strength and appropriate His armor: ". . . that ye may be able to stand against the wiles of the devil" (6:11). This strategy is so important to understand that Paul repeated it twice. In 6:13 he admonished, "Wherefore take unto you the whole armour of God, that ye may be able to withstand in the evil day, and having done all, to stand." Again in 6:14 he directly commanded, "Stand therefore. . . ." The picture that Paul presented here is obviously one of *defensive* warfare. Every piece of equipment mentioned in this passage is defensive in nature (with the possible exception of the sword, which could be used either defensively or offensively, depending upon the mission given).

Never in Scripture is the believer exhorted to seek out or attack the Devil or his demons. On the contrary, the Devil seeks to attack the believer. Peter made this clear when he stated, "Be sober, be vigilant; because your adversary the devil, as a roaring lion, walketh about, seeking whom he may devour" (1 Pet. 5:8). The believer has been given his marching orders by God. He is to glorify God in his living and carry out the Great Commission. As he happily carries out these tasks, he will not need to be looking for Satan; Satan will be looking for him! So then, when Satan attacks, the believer is to stand firm, being protected by the full armor of God. Peter said that the appropriate response of the believer is to ". . . resist stedfast in the faith" (1 Pet 5:9). The admonition of James is "Submit yourselves therefore to God. Resist the devil, and he will flee from you" (James 4:7). When the believer firmly resists Satan while clad in the armor of God, Satan will flee. The believer will then continue to march forward, carrying out the commands given him by his Heavenly Captain.

This Biblical picture is unfortunately often ignored today. Popular books and articles often tell the Christian to engage in aggressive spiritual warfare, to attack Satan and to give the Devil his due. Many well-meaning but misled believers have accordingly laid their proper spiritual priorities aside and become preoccupied with demons, Satan, exorcism and engagement of the powers of darkness. Warfare with Satan is quite real, and it is the experience of every believer at some time or other. However, God's plan is for the Christian to resist attack when it comes instead of looking for demonic forces to battle. To lose this perspective is both unwise and dangerous.

Our Fearsome Enemy

Underestimating the Enemy is a tactical error in battle that inevitably leads to a crushing defeat. Anyone familiar with sports, for example, has seen this fact illustrated many times. Who has not cringed at some time or another when his favorite team, picked to win handily against an alleged inferior opponent, ended up losing due to failure to take that opponent seriously? Just as careless preparation and a nonchalant attitude can rob a team of victory in the athletic realm, the same attitude can also prove disastrous in the spiritual realm. Paul wanted the believer to have no illusions concerning the nature of his Enemy; therefore he described him carefully in Ephesians 6:11 and 12. This passage reveals four characteristics of the Enemy. First, he is crafty. Paul referred to the "wiles of the devil." The Greek word for wiles is *methodeias*, and means "scheming, craftiness . . . strategems."[1] It is related to the verb form *methodeuō*, which means to "defraud, deceive, pervert."[2] The words are compound words, coming from a combination of *meta* (meaning "after") and *duos* (meaning "a way"). The idea, therefore, is of a way of going after something, or a method.[3] The word acquired an evil sense and suggests the idea of accomplishing evil designs with trickery, ingenuity or subtle craftiness. Our Enemy is immensely deceptive and crafty, and we must therefore be alert and careful to measure all things by the standard of the Word of God. Persuasive speakers, powerful associations and experiences can all be used as manipulative tools of Satan to sidetrack and devastate believers.

Second, the Enemy is vicious. Paul stated in 6:12 that the believer *wrestles* against these forces. In choosing the word "wrestle" (*palē*), Paul drew a picture from the athletic contests of his day. In a Greek wrestling match, the contestant would attempt to win by throwing his opponent to the ground and pinning him, holding him down with his hand over the opponent's neck. The loser could then have his eyes gouged out.[4] Thus the picture is of personal hand-to-hand combat, with much at stake. The demonic forces of Satan delight in spiritually maiming and devastating the children of God. Given the opportunity to take the upper hand in a believer's life, demons will certainly do it. Therefore the believer needs to take the battle seriously and yield no ground to the Adversary through sinful, rebellious living.

Third, the Enemy is formidable. The believer is not locked in spiritual combat against a flesh-and-blood enemy (6:12). The Enemy therefore does not ultimately consist of people who oppose the Person or work of Christ, but rather in the demonic forces of "spiritual wickedness in high places." Because of this, the believer's weapons of warfare must not be carnal (2 Cor. 10:3–5), but spiritual. Being personal spirit beings, demons are formidable foes that must be defeated on a spiritual level, in the power of God.

The formidable nature of the Enemy is further observed when one sees that it is an organized foe that the believer faces. This seems to be the idea behind the words "principalities . . . powers" in Ephesians 6:12. Satan's forces apparently have various positions or ranks, with corresponding authority given to them by their evil master to carry out their nefarious assignments. The believer is therefore not facing a disorganized Enemy that attacks haphazardly.

Paul's description of the satanic host as "the rulers of the darkness of this world" gives yet another glimpse of the formidable power that the Enemy has. A better translation of the phrase would be "world-rulers of this darkness." The term "world-rulers" (*kosmokratoras*) is a compound Greek term, coming from the words *kosmos* (meaning "world") and *kratos* (meaning "might, strength").[5] The idea, then, is of satanic powers who have the might to exercise rulership over the world system that is opposed to God. These words bring out the terrifying power of their influence and the comprehensiveness of their plans, and thus emphasize again the seriousness of the battle.[6]

Fourth, the Enemy is wicked. Paul described the forces of Satan as "spiritual wickedness in high places." As a wicked foe, the Enemy will use any means of deception, manipulation or attack to attempt to destroy the usefulness and testimony of the child of

God. Christians may be absolutely assured that no ultimate good ever comes from compromising with satanic forces, yielding spiritual ground to them or deliberately putting oneself into their territory through such careless things as dabbling with the occult.

Our Great Provision

With such an awesome description of the power and character of the Enemy, it is a comfort to know that God has indeed provided the means by which the believer may have full safety and victory. The means involves putting on the full armor of God. Paul admonished, "Wherefore take unto you the whole armour of God, that ye may be able to withstand in the evil day, and having done all, to stand" (Eph. 6:13).

But what is this armor? Much debate and discussion have been generated by this question, but Paul himself seems to supply the answer in Romans 13:12 and 14. He stated:

> The night is far spent, the day is at hand: let us therefore cast off the works of darkness, and let us put on the armour of light. . . . But put ye on the Lord Jesus Christ, and make not provision for the flesh, to fulfill [its] lusts.

A clear twofold link exists between this passage and the admonition to put on the whole armor of God in Ephesians 6:13. First, we see a similarity of ideas; both passages speak of putting on a figurative armor. Second, we find a similarity of terminology in the word "put on" (*enduō*), which is used in the aorist middle form in Ephesians 6:13, Romans 13:12 and 13:14.[7] The vital link between these passages is thus established, showing that putting on the armor of God is equivalent to putting on Christ.

This idea of putting on Christ may be understood in two senses. One of them is a positional sense, in which a person puts on Christ by trusting Christ as his personal Savior. Apart from this we have no sufficient armor of defense against the Adversary. Scripture clearly teaches that the unbeliever is part of a world system that "lieth in [the wicked one]" (1 John 5:19). He walks ". . . according to the prince of the power of the air, the spirit that now worketh in the [sons] of disobedience" (Eph. 2:1, 2) and his spiritual father is the Devil (John 8:44), who supernaturally blinds his mind lest he believe the gospel (2 Cor. 4:4).

However, when one trusts Christ as his Savior he is a partaker "of the inheritance of the saints in light" (Col. 1:12). God has "delivered [him] from the power of darkness" and has "translated [him] into the kingdom of his dear Son: In whom [the believer] has redemption through his blood" (Col. 1:13, 14). Being in Christ, he is a new creation (2 Cor. 5:17); and being identified permanently with Christ in His death, burial and resurrection, he is dead to sin and alive to God (Rom. 6:3–11). Thus every provision is made by which victory over Satan and his forces may be a reality in every believer's life.

However, Paul was writing to those who were *already* believers. As believers, they had previously put on Christ in a positional way. Thus when Paul commanded them to put on Christ by putting on the armor of God, he must have meant something more than simply trusting Christ as Savior—something that those who are *already believers* are obligated to do. That "something" includes the practical appropriation of Christ in the believer's life, which is accomplished by knowing one's position of being identified fully with Christ in His death, burial and resurrection (Rom. 6:3–10), reckoning oneself to be dead therefore to sin and alive to God (Rom. 6:11, 12), and consciously yielding oneself to Christ rather than to sin (Rom. 6:13–23). The verb "put on" (*enduō*) has the idea of drawing on something or clothing oneself with something.[8] The believer's act of putting on the armor, then, involves clothing himself with the character of Christ by consciously yielding to Him and drawing upon His strength for victory.

Paul began his description of the armor by referring to the military belt or girdle. He said, "Stand therefore, having your loins [girded] about with truth" (Eph. 6:14). The belt was usually made of leather, often studded with nails. It was important because it carried the soldier's sword or dagger and also acted as a support, giving the soldier freedom of activity.[9] Its spiritual counterpart is "truth," that is, truthfulness, sincerity or personal integrity. This must characterize the believer's relationships with self, others and God. The believer must harbor no duplicity or deceit in his life if he is to win the battle. To be otherwise produces a moral and spiritual weakness that the Adversary can exploit, leading to spiritual defeat. To put on the girdle of truth, the believer must confess all sham and deceit in his Christian life, denounce it as unacceptable behavior and appropriate the Christlike characteristic of truthfulness in all of his relationships.

The next item of armor that Paul mentioned is the "breastplate of righteousness." The Roman soldier's breastplate could take one of two forms: either a metal plate or a coat of mail that covered the heart and chest. It was designed to protect the heart and other vital organs. Its spiritual counterpart consists of personal holiness or uprightness of life, which is actively accomplished when the believer yields himself to God as an instrument of righteousness. Elsewhere (Rom. 6:13) Paul stated:

> Neither yield ye your members as instruments of unrighteousness unto sin: but yield yourselves unto God, as those that are alive from the dead, and your members as instruments of righteousness unto God.

When a believer allows sin to have dominion over him by yielding to it and tolerating it in his life, he is like a soldier without a breastplate. He leaves an open opportunity for the Enemy to inflict serious spiritual wounds in his life.

Paul's next focus of attention is upon the soldier's footwear. He exhorts the believer to have his "feet shod with the preparation of the gospel of peace." The historical reference is to the heavy spiked or ribbed soles on the Roman soldier's sandals, along with his shin-guards. These sandals not only protected the soldier's feet, but they also enabled him to step surely and confidently, even in slippery places. While some have seen the reference here to the obligation of the believer to carry the gospel to others, the most probable meaning of this phrase involves the believer's readiness and calm assurance in the face of attack, due to the gospel of peace. The good news that the Christian has peace with God through the finished work of Christ (Rom. 5:1) gives him a confident calmness, so that he may march forward for God unafraid, no matter what circumstances may come his way. A spirit of fear can be a devastating deterrent to victorious living and can be seriously exploited by the Adversary. Instead of a spirit of fear, the believer should display a spirit of power, love and a sound mind (2 Tim. 1:7). As he walks in obedience to God, he knows that the God of peace is with him (Phil. 4:9).

The shield of faith is Paul's next center of attention. He admonished, "Above all, taking the shield of faith, wherewith ye shall be able to quench all the fiery darts of the wicked [one]" (Eph. 6:16). The word "shield" that is used here (*thureon*) is closely related to the Greek word *thura*, meaning "a door." It was, in fact, shaped somewhat like a door, being about two and one-half feet wide and four feet high. It had a wood frame, was covered with leather and could be used by the Roman soldier as either a sort of roof or wall before him. The shield was needed to protect the soldiers from such things as "fiery darts," or arrows that were dipped in burning pitch before being shot.

The spiritual counterpart of the shield is the faith of the believer. The Christian is to walk by faith, not by sight (2 Cor. 5:7). It is ever so tempting for the believer to live his life under an emotional sway. As Satan fires his deadly darts of difficult circumstances, temptation, disappointment, impurity or criticism, believers are apt to react emotionally. They may follow their feelings and be defeated. The counteraction to this is to hold forth the shield of faith; meaning that the believer reacts by taking God at His Word and reckoning it to be true in his life. He reckons that Christ has provided victory and acts upon His truth. The result is that the darts of Satan do not harm him but fall harmlessly to the earth.

"Take the helmet of salvation" is the next admonition of Paul. Among the pieces of the Roman armor, the helmet was one of the most notable and decorative. It consisted of a gleaming metal cap, often with a decorative crest, and it protected the head of the soldier from blows such as those delivered with a battle ax. The spiritual application of this involves a proper knowledge and appropriation of one's salvation in Christ. Just as the helmet protected the head or mind of the Roman soldier, so a proper knowledge of salvation in Christ protects the mind of the believer from the blows of Satan. This knowledge may include several things. It may include an objective knowledge of what the believer is and has in Christ. A person who is clear on this doctrine has laid a firm foundation for general doctrinal soundness. The ignorance of many believers concerning the doctrine of salvation is both tragic and dangerous, and Satan has led many astray into false doctrine as a result. This knowledge may also include a subjective knowledge of salvation—the believer's assurance that he is truly born again and is being kept by the power of God. A constant worrying about whether one is saved or whether he has lost his salvation is a serious obstacle indeed to victory over Satan and his demonic hordes.

The final piece of armor listed by Paul is the "sword of the Spirit, which is the word of God." The sword mentioned here is the small hand sword that the Roman soldier attached to his belt. It was about eighteen inches long, two-edged and pointed. It was used for piercing and hacking. The spiritual application of the use of the Word of God in defensive warfare is, of course, best seen in the temptation of Christ by Satan in Matthew 4:1–10. When confronted three times by satanic temptation, Christ answered with a firm "It is written" and won the victory. If the Christian is to achieve real victory over Satan and his evil cohorts, he must have a good working knowledge of Scripture—a knowledge that will enable him to stand firm when Satan tempts. Sadly, the knowledge of Scripture that some believers possess is largely theoretical in nature. Abstract doctrinal ideas are memorized for theology exams or church membership interviews; but people often have an inability to correlate and apply those ideas to practical Christian living, where frequent, close combat with the enemy takes place. An earnest Christian who has hidden the Word of God in his heart and who can apply it skillfully and accurately will thwart any attempt of the Enemy to inflict spiritual damage in his life.

Having described in detail the armor of God, Paul finally gave the circumstances under which it is put on—prayer and watchfulness. He stated, "Praying always with all prayer and supplication in the Spirit, and watching thereunto with all perseverance and supplication for all saints" (Eph. 6:18). The words "praying" (*proseuchomenoi*) and "watching" (*agrupnountes*) can be called circumstantial participles in the Greek, meaning that they give the circumstances under which the armor of God is put on. Furthermore, they are in the present tense, meaning that these things should be consistently attended to in the warfare of the believer. The prayer closet could thus aptly be called the armor room. It is here that the Christian yields himself to God, cries out to Him for strength for the battle and develops the attitude of humble dependence upon Him that is necessary for victory.

The believer also remembers that he can never let up and set the armor aside—not even for a minute. Thus his prayer life must be vigilant, and he must be ever watching. The word "watching" literally means "to keep oneself awake, be on the alert."[10] The believer, then, is ever to be on the alert in his walk, ever awake and mindful for himself and others as he seeks to serve God, and ever instant in prayer as he puts on the armor of God. It is with this in mind that the believer is told in 1 Thessalonians 5:6–8:

> Therefore let us not sleep, as do others; but let us watch and be sober. For they that sleep sleep in the night; and they that [are drunk] are [drunk] in the night. But let us, who are of the day, be sober, putting on the breastplate of faith and love; and for an helmet, the hope of salvation.

So, then, the believer who humbly avails himself of the power of God and appropriates His full armor in his life in connection with prayer and watchfulness is more than a match for the Adversary. This is the plan of God for victory over the powers of darkness.

DEALING WITH SUSPECTED DEMON POSSESSION

Probably no genuine believers would argue against the necessity of putting on the armor of God to win the battle against Satan and his wicked cohorts. What does one do, however, when he comes upon a person who is suspected of being demonized? What is the proper procedure to follow? Now that a proper understanding of the nature of the protection and victory that God provides in Christ has been established, these questions can be answered Biblically.

The Proper Diagnosis

To begin with, one must be exceedingly careful not to diagnose demon possession wrongly. Generally speaking, cases of demon possession will be far less common today than they were in the Gospel period. As pointed out in chapter two, the period of Jesus' earthly ministry involved a titanic battle between the King and His associates, and Satan and his demons. The kingdom of heaven was at hand, and the house of the strongman, Satan, was being plundered. The early Church Age described in Acts was seemingly more quiet and reserved by comparison as far as demon possession was concerned, especially as time went on. Scripture is silent on the issue of the extent of demon possession in the present time; but if this malady suits Satan's purposes and a *willing* victim is available, we have no reason to suppose that demon possession cannot presently take place.

It should be recalled that historically most cases of demon possession described in the New Testament occurred in idolatrous or occultic settings such as Galilee, Phoenicia or Ephesus. It seems reasonable to conclude from this that demon possession is most likely to be encountered in persons whose past involves serious involvement with the occult or idolatry. Because these practices are so directly and immediately involved with demons, they provide a convenient opening for possible demonization.

Even past involvement with idolatry or the occult provides no guarantee, however, that a person is demon-possessed. After all, thousands of Old Testament Israelites became involved in idolatry and the occult but were still evidently not demon-possessed. Therefore one should be extremely careful to eliminate all other explanations for the behavior of the afflicted person before calling him demonized.

It has been demonstrated in chapter five that the Bible provides no tests that can be used to determine demon possession. Nor is there a gift of discerning spirits that gives certain individuals supernatural knowledge to know if a person is demonized. Furthermore, it is unbiblical to test people who are not *clearly* demonized to find "hidden demons." The only recorded cases of demon possession that Jesus and the apostles dealt with were obvious ones—cases so clear that even the unregenerate could recognize the malady.

The historical record in the Gospels suggests three main symptoms of demon possession. In rare cases where a demonized person is confronted, he may display (1) a combination of the symptoms of physical malady (often extreme), (2) the distinct presence of another personality—displayed by speaking in another voice in an intelligent and coherent way (which is *not* true of so-called mental illnesses such a schizophrenia) and (3) clairvoyance, meaning supernatural knowledge, particularly in spiritual matters. One must be careful, however, not to brand people recklessly as demon-possessed. In cases of real Biblical demon possessions, the problem should be obvious.

The Road to Victory

When considering the Biblical road to victory over Satan and demonic forces, one must begin by realizing the ultimate victory can be found *only* in the provision of God—namely, the armor that He has provided. Exorcism neither gets to the root of the problem nor provides an ultimate solution. This is perhaps best illustrated once again in the instructions of Paul to the church at Ephesus. Here was a church situated in a town that was famous as a center for both the occult and idolatry. The Ephesian temple dedicated to the cult of Artemis (Acts 19:23–41) was one of the seven wonders of the ancient world, and the occultic scripts produced there were famous.[11] Paul's greatest acts of casting out demons took place there (Acts 19:11–22). Yet when he wrote to the Ephesian believers in detail concerning how to achieve victory over Satan and demonic forces, he gave no instructions whatsoever concerning exorcism. Astonishingly, he never even mentioned it!

It is suggested here that one reason Paul excluded expulsion of demons in his instructions was that it is at best a marginal ministry objective. It does not provide the ultimate solution to victory over demonic forces. It was pointed out earlier that the chief value of the demon expulsions performed by Jesus and the apostles was that they were sign-miracles. They authenticated the claims of Jesus to messiahship and deity, and the apostles as His special representatives. Apart from this, casting out demons had only limited value. The Lord Himself warned that if an unclean spirit goes out of a person and his life remains empty, a worse demonic invasion may take place, with the result that the person is actually worse off than he was (Matt. 12:43–45).

In dealing with people who have demonic problems, including suspected demonic possession, the proper course of action is to challenge them to put on Christ. The connection of Ephesians 6:11 with Romans 13:12 and 14 makes it clear that this is the meaning of putting on the armor of God. For the unbeliever, Christ must be put on positionally; this means his turning to Christ as his personal Savior. This is the only true and ultimate solution for his problems with demons. Apart from putting on Christ, the unbeliever remains in Satan's realm and has no ultimate defense against renewed demonic attack, even if the demons have been previously cast out. When a person turns to Christ as his Savior, he is translated automatically into the kingdom of God. The Lord may thus be counted upon to free His new child from the control of Satan, including possession (Col. 1:13, 14; 2 Cor. 5:17).

If in rare cases efforts to witness to a demonized person are impossible due to the severity of demonic attack, the mature believer may pray, calling upon Jesus to forcibly expel the demon. (Such prayer would not include dangerous practices such as talking to demons or probing for "hidden demons.") It has been shown that deliverance from demon possession could be regarded as a kind of healing, since the primary manifestation of Biblical demon possession was physical malady. The *gift* of healing was associated with the apostles as a sign-gift. Every believer today, however, has the privilege of praying for healing. Thus if the fact of demon possession has been clearly established in a victim, godly, consecrated believers may fervently pray for divine compulsion.

For the believer, problems due to demonic influence result from a refusal to put on Christ in his life and walk. Rather than appropriating the Person and work of Christ by relying upon His power, yielding to Him and obeying His Word, this believer consciously yields himself to the demonic, with disastrous results. For this believer, the need is to explain the nature of his sin, exhort him to repent of it, and then teach him to avail himself of the provision of the armor of God in Christ.

Once a person has been freed from demonic control, he should immediately destroy all items related to the occult or idolatry. When many people in Ephesus were saved out of occultic backgrounds (and some of them had been demon-possessed; Acts

19:11, 12, 18–20), they came forth and confessed their deeds, destroying their occultic literature. Accordingly, idolatrous connections must be broken (1 Cor. 10:14, 15; 1 John 5:21). Idols should be destroyed and attendance at idolatrous feasts and functions must be avoided, for "Ye cannot drink the cup of the Lord, and the cup of [demons]" (1 Cor. 10:21). In like manner, all occultic objects and associations must be discarded. Ouija boards, tarot cards, items used in satanic worship, and occultic literature cannot be tolerated, nor can occultic friendships or attendance at events where mediumistic or occultic activities take place. To claim Christ as Lord and Savior while one continues to tolerate these things not only involves casting aside one's only source of protection from satanic forces, but it also includes provoking the Lord to jealousy (1 Cor. 10:22). The life, in short, must be yielded to Christ, and absolutely no vestige of demonized religion or practices can be tolerated.

SUMMARY

Exorcism does not provide the ultimate answer for deliverance from the demonic; hence the Bible gives no Pauline instruction concerning how to diagnose demon possession or cast out demons. There is, however, extensive discussion in Ephesians 6:10–20 concerning how the believer can obtain victory over demonic forces. God's plan of victory involves three things: reliance upon God's strength, putting on the whole armor of God and waging a defensive strategy. The believer is to march forth carrying out the Lord's commands, and he is to stand firm when attacked by Satan. His attention is to be centered upon Christ and His will, rather than seeking to battle with Satan. The enemy is never to be taken lightly. Satan and his demons are intelligent, powerful and resourceful foes. If ever a believer seeks to achieve victory over them with his own strength or methods, he will surely fail. Therefore the believer needs to be clad in the armor of God. According to Ephesians 6:11 as compared with Romans 13:12 and 14, the armor is Christ.

Putting on Christ should be thought of in a twofold manner. First, it involves the assumption that the individual has trusted Christ as his personal Savior. This is a positional putting on of

Christ. Second, it involves a practical appropriation of Christ in a believer's daily life. This appropriation includes the active yielding of one's members as instruments of righteousness unto God, an affirming knowledge of one's position in Christ and a practical use of Scripture to put the Adversary to flight. Once Christ has been "put on" by faith, no quarter, place or opportunity can be given to the enemy. Therefore all occultic or idolatrous associations or items must be discarded or destroyed. In their place, identification and involvement with God's people through the local church should be practiced as one grows in the grace and knowledge of the Lord.

The great demonic expulsions that Christ accomplished so dramatically in His public ministry show His full authority over the powers of darkness. He is the believer's great armor of protection; and no more sufficient armor is needed! In Him believers have victory, and yielded believers need not fear the enemy.

LIST OF ABBREVIATIONS

BAGD W. Bauer, W. F. Arndt, and F. W. Gingrich, *Greek-English Lexicon of the New Testament*

BDB F. Brown, S. R. Driver, and C. A. Briggs, *Hebrew and English Lexicon of the Old Testament*

ICC *International Critical Commentary*

NIC *New International Commentary of the New Testament*

NTC *New Testament Commentary*

TDNT G. Kittel and G. Friedrich (eds.), *Theological Dictionary of the New Testament*

END NOTES

INTRODUCTION

[1] Rodger K. Bufford, *Counseling and the Demonic*, Resources for Christian Counseling, ed. Gary R. Collins (Dallas: Word Books, 1988), p. 18.

[2] Tipper Gore, *Raising PG Kids in an X-Rated Society* (Nashville: Abingdon Press, 1987), p. 118.

[3] Ibid., p. 119.

[4] Bufford, *Counseling*, p. 18.

[5] Gore, *PG Kids*, p. 118.

[6] Dave Hunt and T. A. McMahon, *The Seduction of Christianity: Spiritual Discernment in the Last Days* (Eugene, OR: Harvest House Publishers, 1985), p. 8.

[7] Bufford, *Counseling*, p. 18.

[8] Ibid., p. 17.

[9] For examples of this, see Kenneth E. Hagin, *The Satan, Demons, and Demon Possession Series*, 4 vols. (Tulsa, OK: Kenneth Hagin Ministries, 1983).

[10] Merrill Frederick Unger, *Biblical Demonology* (Wheaton, IL: Van Kampen Press, 1952), p. 100.

[11] Merrill Frederick Unger, *Demons in the World Today* (Wheaton, IL: Tyndale House Publishers, 1971), p. 59.

[12] C. Fred Dickason, *Demon Possession and the Christian: A New Perspective* (Chicago: Moody Press, 1987), p. 175.

[13] Mark I. Bubeck, *The Adversary: The Christian Verses Demonic Activity* (Chicago: Moody Press, 1975), p. 86.

[14] Ibid., pp. 117–22.

[15] Peter Masters, *The Healing Epidemic* (London: The Wakeman Trust, 1988), pp. 100–11.

[16] Ibid., pp. 87, 88.

[17] Ibid., pp. 89–93.

[18] Ibid., pp. 94–98.

[19] Ibid., pp. 91, 92.

CHAPTER 1

[1] Bufford, *Counseling*, pp. 104–5.

[2] Ibid., pp. 49–50, 104–6, 118–20.

[3] Kent Philpott, *A Manual of Demonology and the Occult* (Grand Rapids: Zondervan Publishing House, 1973), pp. 127–28. See also Dickason, *Possession*, p. 164.

[4] Dickason, *Possession*, pp. 161, 164–65.

[5] *TDNT*, s.v. *"echō,"* by Hermann Hanse, 2:821–22.

[6] Henry Joseph Thayer, *A Greek-English Lexicon of the New Testament* (New York: American Book Co., 1889), pp. 266–67.

[7] Thayer, *Lexicon*, p. 266.

[8] Daniel A. Hern, "Demonology and the Believer" (M.Div. thesis, Grace Theological Seminary, 1978), pp. 6–9.

[9] Lewis Sperry Chafer, *Satan: His Motive and Methods*, new and revised ed. (Chicago: Moody Press, 1918), p. 64.

[10] Bufford, *Counseling*, p. 48.

[11] For a thorough discussion of the etymology of "demonized," see Dickason, *Possession*, pp. 37, 38.

[12] Ibid.

[13] Edward Langton, *Essentials of Demonology* (London: The Epworth Press, 1949), p. 152.

[14] See the Book of Tobit 6:7 ff.; and 2 Maccabees 5:41.

[15] James Hope Moulton and George Milligan, *The Vocabulary of the Greek Testament Illustrated from the Papyri and Other Non-Literary Sources* (Grand Rapids: Wm. B. Eerdmans Publishing Co., 1930), pp. 464–70.

[16] BAGD, p. 605.

[17] H. K. Luce, "The Gospel According to St. Luke," in *The Cambridge Greek Testament for Schools and Colleges*, ed., A. Nairne (Cambridge: The Cambridge University Press, 1949), p. 216. Also George Arthur Buttrick, ed., *The Interpreter's Bible*, 12 vols. (New York: Abingdon Press, 1951), 7:404.

[18] Charles R. Smith, "The New Testament Doctrine of Demons," *Grace Journal*, 10 (Spring 1969):38.

[19] Thayer, *Lexicon*, p. 40.

[20] Ibid.

[21] Richard Chenevix Trench, *Synonyms of the New Testament* (Grand Rapids: Associated Publishers and Authors, n.d.), p. 137.

[22] Unger, *Biblical Demonology*, p. 105.

[23] Merrill F. Unger, *What Demons Can Do to Saints* (Chicago: Moody Press, 1977), p. 112. See also Millard J. Erickson, *Christian Theology*, 3 vols. (Grand Rapids: Baker Book House, 1983), 1:449.

[24] Unger, *Saints*, pp. 51, 73. See also Dickason, *Possession*, pp. 218, 225.

[25] Langton, *Demonology*, p. 149. See also William M. Taylor, *The Miracles of Our Savior Expounded and Illustrated*, 10th ed. (New York: A. C. Armstrong & Son, 1910), p. 217.

26 Erickson, *Theology*, 1:449.

27 Millard J. Sall, "Demon Possession or Psychopathology? A Clinical Differentiation," *Journal of Psychology and Theology*, 4 (Fall 1976):288.

28 Ibid., pp. 288–89.

29 This does not mean, however, that demons are omniscient. Demons are able to "predict" some future events successfully because those events are planned in secret by Satan and his demonic subordinates. Demons already know what they plan to do in these events and may communicate that knowledge in the form of "foretelling the future" to a few unsuspecting persons. This is not, however, the same as omniscience. Omniscience is an attribute of God alone.

30 William Menzies Alexander, *Demonic Possession in the New Testament: Its Relation—Historical, Medical and Theological* (Edinburgh: T & T Clark, 1902), p. 125.

31 For an exposition of this view, see Unger, *Saints*, pp. 51, 73.

32 Kurt E. Koch, *Demonology Past and Present* (Grand Rapids: Kregel Publications, 1973), pp. 141–47.

33 Dickason, *Possession*, p. 192.

34 Unger, *Biblical Demonology*, p. 95.

35 Dickason, *Possession*, p. 225.

36 Ibid., p. 286.

37 John J. Davis, *Demons, Exorcism and the Evangelical* (Winona Lake, IN: BMH Books, 1977), p. 8.

38 Willem Berends, "The Biblical Criteria for Demon Possession," *The Westminster Theological Journal*, 37 (Spring 1975): 342–65.

39 Langton, *Demonology*, pp. 178–80.

40 F. F. Bruce, *Commentary on the Book of Acts*, NIC (Grand Rapids:

Wm. B. Eerdmans Publishing Co., 1975), pp. 391–92.

[41] However, some claim that King Saul was demon-possessed. See Dickason, *Possession*, pp. 121–23; Bufford, *Counseling*, pp. 36, 37.

[42] John White, "Problems and Procedures in Exorcism," in *Demon Possession: A Medical, Historical, Anthropological and Theological Symposium*, ed. John Warwick Montgomery (Minneapolis, MN: Bethany Fellowship, 1976), p. 282.

[43] Theodore Graebner, "Demoniacal Possession," *Concordia Theological Monthly*, 4 (August 1933):589.

[44] Richard Chenevix Trench, *Notes on the Miracles of Our Lord* (Westwood, NJ: Fleming H. Revell Co., 1953), p. 166.

[45] Lewis Sperry Chafer, *Systematic Theology*, 7 vols. (Dallas: Dallas Seminary Press, 1947), 2:210.

[46] Unger, *Saints*, pp. 139–40.

CHAPTER 2

[1] A. A. Hodge, *Outlines in Theology* (New York: A. C. Armstrong and Son, 1891), p. 257.

[2] This is the view of Keim, as explained in Alexander, *Possession*, pp. 140–41.

[3] Michael Wilson, "Exorcism: A Clinical/Pastoral Practice Which Raises Serious Questions," *Expository Times*, 86 (July 1975):293.

[4] Martin Ebon, *The Devil's Bride: Exorcism Past and Present* (New York: Harper & Row Publishers, 1974), p. 27.

[5] Juan B. Cortes and Florence M. Gatti, *The Case against Possessions and Exorcisms* (New York: Vantage Press, 1975), p. 138.

[6] David Lyon Bartlett, "Exorcism Stories in the Gospel of Mark" (Ph.D. dissertation, Yale University, 1972).

[7] BAGD, p. 277.

[8] Cortes and Gatti, *Possessions*, p. 117.

[9] Ibid. See also BAGD, p. 227.

[10] Josephus, *Antiquities of the Jews*, 8. 2.5.

[11] M. J. Baker, "Possession and the Occult—A Psychiatrist's View," *Churchman*, 94 (May, 1980):246.

[12] William L. Lane, trans., *The Gospel According to Mark*, NIC (Grand Rapids: Wm. B. Eerdmans Publishing Co., 1974), p. 70.

[13] Unger, *Saints*, p. 130.

[14] Cited by Robert H. Culpepper, *Evaluating the Charismatic Movement: A Theological and Biblical Appraisal* (Valley Forge, PA: Judson Press, 1977), p. 131.

[15] Hagin, *Possession Series*, 4:20.

[16] Dickason, *Possession*, pp. 188–91. However, Dickason would not claim that he is casting out demons as Jesus did.

[17] Ibid., p. 205.

[18] John Warwick Montgomery, "Exorcism: Is It for Real?" *Christianity Today* (July 26, 1974): 6–8.

[19] Ibid.

[20] Unger, *Saints*, p. 152. See also Dickason, *Possession*, pp. 184, 207.

[21] James Oliver Buswell, *A Systematic Theology of the Christian Religion*, one volume ed., reprinted (Grand Rapids: Zondervan Publishing House, 1981), p. 176.

[22] *TDNT*, s.v. "*daimōn, daimonion*," by Werner Foerster, 2:18. See also Graham Dow, "The Case for the Existence of Demons," *Churchman* 94 (May, 1980): 200.

[23] Unger, *Demons in the World*, p. 190.

[24] Cortes and Gatti, *Possessions*, pp. 119–20.

[25] Lane, *Mark*, p. 177.

[26] G. Campbell Morgan, *The Gospel According to Mark* (Old Tappan, NJ: Fleming H. Revell Co., 1927), p. 103.

[27] Henry Barclay Swete, *Commentary on Mark* (Grand Rapids: Kregel Publications, 1977), p. 90.

[28] James D. G. Dunn and Graham H. Twelftree, "Demon-Possession and Exorcism in the New Testament," *Churchman*, 94 (May 1980): 220.

[29] Richard H. Hiers, "Satan, Demons and the Kingdom of God," *Scottish Journal of Theology*, 37 (February 1974): 42, 43.

[30] Richard H. Hiers, *The Kingdom of God in the Synoptic Traditions*, University of Florida Humanities Monograph Number 3 (Gainesville, Florida: University of Florida Press, 1970), pp. 42–47.

[31] Ibid.

[32] Hiers, "Kingdom of God," p. 47.

[33] BAGD, p. 303.

[34] Howard Clark Kee, "The Terminology of Mark's Exorcism Stories," *New Testament Studies*, 14 (January 1968): 238–39.

[35] Ibid.

[36] Ibid.

[37] Ibid., pp. 239–42.

[38] Hiers, *Synoptic Traditions*, p. 39.

[39] Ibid.

[40] Anton Fredricksen, "The Conflict of Jesus with Unclean Spirits," *Theology: A Journal of Historic Christianity*, 22 (March 1931): 128.

[41] Davis, *Demons*, p. 6.

[42] Taylor, *Miracles*, p. 218.

CHAPTER 3

[1] Norval Geldenhuys, *Supreme Authority: The Authority of the Lord, His Apostles and the New Testament* (Grand Rapids: Wm. B. Eerdmans Publishing Co., 1953), p. 47.

[2] G. Abbott-Smith, *A Manual Greek Lexicon of the New Testament* (New York: Charles Scribner's Sons, 1921), pp. 54, 55.

[3] BAGD, p. 99.

[4] *TDNT*, s.v. "*apostellō*," pp. 414, 15.

[5] Ibid.

[6] Ibid.

[7] Ibid., pp. 420–21.

[8] Charles R. Smith, *Tongues in Biblical Perspective: A Summary of Biblical Conclusions Concerning Tongues*, 2d ed. (revised) (Winona Lake, IN: BMH Books, 1973), p. 61.

[9] Homer A. Kent, Jr., *The Freedom of God's Sons: Studies In Galatians* (Winona Lake, IN: BMH Books, 1976), pp. 27, 28.

[10] Cited in Peter Masters and John C. Whitcomb, *The Charismatic Phenomenon* (London: The Metropolitan Tabernacle, Elephant & Castle, 1980), pp. 12, 13.

[11] BAGD, p. 755.

[12] *TDNT*, s.v. "*sēmeion*," by Karl Heinrich Rengstorf, 7:202–5.

[13] Ibid., 7:203.

[14] The translation is from Smith, *Tongues*, p. 71.

[15] R.C.H. Lenski, *The Interpretation of St. Mark's Gospel*, reprint ed. (Minneapolis, MN: Augsburg Publishing House, 1964), pp. 240, 243–44.

[16] Carl Brumbeck, *Suddenly from Heaven* (Springfield, MO: Gospel Publishing House, 1961), p. 54.

[17] See Kurt Aland, Matthew Black, Carlo M. Martini, Bruce M. Metzger and Allen Wickgren, eds., *The Greek New Testament*, 2d ed. (New York: United Bible Societies, 1966), p. 196.

[18] Archibald Thomas Robertson, *Word Pictures in the New Testament*, 6 vols. (Nashville, TN: Broadman Press, 1930), 1:4–12.

[19] Ibid., 1:262.

[20] Masters and Whitcomb, *Charismatic Phenomenon*, p. 15.

[21] Swete, *Mark*, p. 405.

[22] Robert Glenn Gromacki, *The Modern Tongues Movement* (Philadelphia: Presbyterian and Reformed Publishing Co., 1967), p. 75.

[23] Bruce, *Acts*, p. 389.

[24] Ibid., p. 389.

[25] Implied by G. Campbell Morgan, *The Gospel According to Matthew* (New York: Fleming H. Revell Co., 1929), p. 225.

[26] J. Macaulay, *Behold Your King* (Chicago: Moody Press, 1952), p. 157.

[27] They include Sinaiticus, Vaticanus and Clement of Alexandria. See Kurt Aland, et al., *The Greek New Testament*, p. 159, note 1.

[28] Swete, *Mark*, p. 202.

[29] Lane, *Mark*, p. 329, note 45; Kurt Aland, et al., *The Greek New Testament*, p. 66, note 4; Alfred Plummer, *An Exegetical Commentary on the Gospel According to St. Matthew* (Grand Rapids: Wm. B. Eerdmans Publishing Co., 1956), p. 243.

[30] Lenski, *Mark*, p. 386.

[31] Plummer, *Matthew*, p. 242.

[32] Lenski, *Mark*, p. 386.

[33] Langton, *Demonology*, p. 174.

[34] This is the date given for Paul's ministry there. See Merrill C. Tenney, *New Testament Times* (Grand Rapids: Wm. B. Eerdmans Publishing Co., 1965), p. 279.

[35] Smith, *Tongues*, p. 66.

[36] Ibid., p. 67.

[37] Ibid., p. 71.

[38] Homer A. Kent, Jr., *The Epistle to the Hebrews* (Winona Lake, IN: BMH Books, 1972), pp. 26, 27.

CHAPTER 4

[1] *Wycliffe Bible Encyclopedia*, s.v. "Seventy Disciples of Our Lord," 2:1557.

[2] Alfred Edersheim, *The Life and Times of Jesus the Messiah*, 1 vol. ed. (Grand Rapids: Wm. B. Eerdmans Publishing Co., 1979), 2:136.

[3] Norval Geldenhuys, *Commentary on the Gospel of Luke*, NIC (Grand Rapids: Wm. B. Eerdmans Publishing Co., 1979), pp. 300–1.

[4] *Wycliffe*, s.v. "Seventy," 2:1557.

[5] Ibid.

[6] Geldenhuys, *Supreme Authority*, pp. 61, 62.

[7] Merrill C. Tenney, "Luke," in *The Wycliffe Bible Commentary*, eds. Charles F. Pfeiffer and Everett F. Harrison (Chicago: Moody Press, 1962), p. 1046.

[8] William C. Kemp, "Did Jesus Cast Out Demons? Mark 12:27" (B.D. monograph, Grace Theological Seminary, 1960), p. 42.

[9] Ibid.

[10] BAGD, p. 841.

[11] R.C.H. Lenski, *The Interpretation of St. Matthew's Gospel*, reprint ed. (Minneapolis, MN: Augsburg Publishing House, 1961), p. 478.

[12] George Eldon Ladd, *Jesus and the Kingdom: The Eschatology of Biblical Realism* (New York: Harper & Row Publishers, 1964), p. 149.

[13] John Pereira, "Jewish Exorcism: a Harmonization of Matthew 12:27 and Acts 19:13–17," (M.Div. thesis, Grace Theological Seminary, 1976), p. 23.

[14] E. H. Plumptre, "The Gospel According to St. Matthew, St. Mark and St. Luke," in vol. 6 of *A Bible Commentary for English Readers*, ed. John Ellicott (London: Casell and Company, n.d.), p. 72.

[15] Edersheim, *Jesus the Messiah*, 2:776.

[16] Pereira, "Jewish Exorcism," p. 31.

[17] Unger, *Biblical Demonology*, pp. 104–5.

[18] Homer A. Kent, Jr., *Jerusalem to Rome: Studies in the Book of Acts* (Winona Lake, IN: BMH Books, 1972), p. 152.

[19] Bruce, *Acts*, p. 390.

[20] Ibid.

[21] W. Denton, *Commentary on the Acts of the Apostles* (London: George Bell and Sons, 1876), p. 181.

[22] Unger, *Biblical Demonology*, p. 105.

[23] Morgan, *Matthew*, p. 79.

[24] M. R. Vincent, "Matthew," in vol. 2 of *Word Studies in the New*

Testament (MacDill AFB, FL: MacDonald Publishing Co., n.d.), p. 36.

[25] C. E. B. Cranfield, *The Gospel According to St. Mark*, 4th ed., revised (Cambridge: Cambridge University Press, 1972), p. 310.

[26] William Hendricksen, *Exposition of the Gospel According to Mark* NTC (Grand Rapids: Baker Book House, 1975), p. 361.

[27] D. Edmond Hiebert, *Mark: A Portrait of the Servant* (Chicago: Moody Press, 1974), p. 230.

[28] Lane, *Mark*, p. 341, note 64.

[29] Ardel B. Caneday, "The Significance and Relationship of the Laying On of Hands and the Bestowal of Spiritual Gifts" (M.Div. thesis, Grace Theological Seminary, 1976), pp. 28, 29.

[30] Smith, *Tongues*, pp. 67, 68.

[31] Ibid., p. 69.

[32] Benjamin B. Warfield, *Counterfeit Miracles* (New York: Charles Scribner's Sons, 1918), p. 22.

[33] H. E. Dana and Julius R. Mantey, *A Manual Grammar of the Greek New Testament* (New York: The MacMillan Company, 1927), p. 102.

[34] Robert G. Gromacki, *New Testament Survey* (Grand Rapids: Baker Book House, 1974), p. 186.

[35] Caneday, "Laying On of Hands," p. 38.

CHAPTER 5

[1] *TDNT*, s.v. "*iaomai*," by Albrecht Oepke, 3:214, 15.

[2] John F. Walvoord, *The Holy Spirit* (Wheaton, IL: Tyndale House Publishers, 1954), p. 180.

[3] Ibid.

⁴ F. W. Grosheide, *Commentary on the First Epistle to the Corinthians*, NIC (Grand Rapids: Wm. B. Eerdmans Publishing Co., 1953), p. 286.

⁵ Abbott-Smith, *Greek Lexicon*, p. 123.

⁶ Charles Hodge, *An Exposition of the First Epistle to the Corinthians* (Grand Rapids: Wm. B. Eerdmans Publishing Co., 1950), p. 247.

⁷ Leopold Sabourin, "The Miracles of Jesus (II): Jesus and the Evil Powers," *Biblical Theology Bulletin*, 4 (June 1974): 172, note 107.

⁸ John F. MacArthur, Jr., *The Charismatics: A Doctrinal Perspective* (Grand Rapids: Zondervan Publishing House, 1978), pp. 132–33.

⁹ Ibid.

¹⁰ This is the view of Habershon, for example. See Ada R. Habershon, The *Study of the Miracles* (Grand Rapids: Kregel Publications, 1957), pp. 242–43.

¹¹ Thomas R. Edgar, "The Cessation of the Sign-Gifts," *Bibliotheca Sacra*, 145 (October-December 1988): 377.

¹² For an example, see Unger, *Saints*, pp. 94–97.

¹³ Grayson H. Ensign and Edward Howe, *Bothered? Bewildered? Bewitched? Your Guide to Practical Supernatural Healing* (Cincinnati, OH: Recovery Publishers, 1984), p. 155, as cited in Dickason, *Possession*, p. 237. See also Rodger K. Bufford's list compiled through research of such literature in Bufford, *Counseling*, pp. 104–8.

¹⁴ Dickason, *Possession*, p. 45.

¹⁵ Bufford, *Counseling*, p. 124.

¹⁶ BAGD, p. 184.

¹⁷ Culpepper, *Charismatic Movement*, p. 128.

¹⁸ Unger, *Biblical Demonology*, p. 98.

¹⁹ Bufford, *Counseling*, pp. 146–47.

[20] See Richard Chenevix Trench, *Notes on the Miracles of Our Lord* (Westwood, NJ: Fleming H. Revell Co., 1953), p. 176.

[21] Walvoord, *The Holy Spirit*, pp. 177–87.

[22] George Mallone, *Those Controversial Gifts* (Downers Grove, IL: InterVarsity Press, 1983), p. 45.

[23] Hodge, *First Corinthians*, p. 248.

[24] Ronald E. Baxter, *Gifts of the Spirit* (Grand Rapids: Kregel Publications, 1983), pp. 112–14.

[25] Cited in Lenski, *First and Second Corinthians*, p. 611.

[26] John F. Walvoord, *The Holy Spirit at Work Today* (Chicago: Moody Press, 1973), p. 53.

[27] J. Stafford Wright, *Christianity and the Occult* (Chicago: Moody Press, 1971), p. 35.

[28] For an example of this in practice, see A. J. MacMillan, *Modern Demon Possession* (Harrisburg, PA: Christian Publications, Inc., n.d.), p. 3. Tim Timmons adds to this other tests, saying that demons will also not acknowledge the deity or shed blood of Christ. See Tim Timmons, *Chains of the Spirit: A Manual for Liberation* (Washington, D.C.: Canon Press, 1973), pp. 57, 58.

[29] Robert Peterson, *Are Demons for Real?* (Chicago: Moody Press, 1972), p. 118.

[30] E. Roger Taylor, "The Identity of the Spirits in 1 John 4:1" (M.Div. thesis, Grace Theological Seminary, 1974), p. 15.

[31] Abbott-Smith, *Greek Lexicon*, p. 120.

[32] Everett F. Harrison, *Introduction to the New Testament* (Grand Rapids: Wm. B. Eerdmans Publishing Co., 1964), p. 412–13.

[33] Kent Philpott, *A Manual of Demonology and the Occult* (Grand Rapids: Zondervan Publishing House, 1974), p. 108.

[34] Abbott-Smith, *Greek Lexicon*, p. 367.

[35] A far more common view of this passage is to understand the "spirits" of 1 John 4:1–4 as a metonymy for the prophets themselves. This view has been championed by, among others, Calvin, Lange, Haupt and Lenski. It is far more acceptable than the idea of linking the "spirits" with demons, and has much in its favor. The following considerations make it problematic, however. (1) The "spirit of antichrist" in 1 John 4:3 is clearly an attitude or disposition. John is contrasting two different attitudes—those that are of God, as opposed to those that are antichrist. He is not contrasting prophets with attitudes. (2) If John was referring to spirits as prophets, it would have been easier to say "test the prophets." (3) If the spirits are simply to be understood as prophets, John was saying that any prophet who made the confession that Christ had come in the flesh was of God. Yet it is conceivable that a man could be correct in this doctrine and still be a false prophet, being a heretic in some other doctrinal area. The approach that equates the "spirits" with the doctrinal attitudes or dispositions of the so-called prophets avoids the above problems, but still links the "spirits" with the prophets themselves. For a fuller explanation relating to the use of "spirit" as a metonymy for the prophets, see John Calvin, "The First Epistle General of John," in vol. 5 of *Calvin's New Testament Commentaries*, trans. by T. H. L. Parker, the trans. ed. by David W. Torrance and Thomas F. Torrance (Grand Rapids: Wm. B. Eerdmans Publishing Co., 1961), p. 284; Erich Haupt, *The First Epistle of John*, trans. by W. B. Pope (Edinburgh: T. & T. Clark, 1879), p. 241; John Peter Lange, "The First Epistle General of John," in vol. 23 of *Commentary on the Holy Scriptures*, trans. and ed. by Philip Schaff (Grand Rapids: Zondervan Publishing House, n.d.), p. 133; R. C. H. Lenski, *The Interpretation of the Epistles of St. Peter, St. John and St. Jude*, reprint ed. (Minneapolis, MN: Augsburg Publishing House, 1966), p. 485.

[36] Unger, *Saints*, p. 59.

[37] For a more extensive description of Satan as a deceiver, see the excellent chapter that J. Dwight Pentecost has written on the subject, in J. Dwight Pentecost, *Your Adversary the Devil* (Grand Rapids: Zondervan Publishing House, 1969), pp. 48–55.

[38] Albert Runge, "Exorcism: A Satanic Ploy?" *His Dominion*, 12 (1987): 14.

[39] Masters, *Healing Epidemic*, pp. 94–98.

⁴⁰ Tom Davis, review of *Demon Possession and the Christian: A New Perspective* by C. Fred Dickason, in *Grace Theological Journal* 10 (Spring 1989): 94.

⁴¹ Sall, "Demon Possession or Psychopathology?" pp. 288–89.

⁴² Alva J. McClain, syllabus for the course "Christian Theology: God and the World," revised by Charles R. Smith, Grace Theological Seminary, Winona Lake, Indiana, 1975, p. 115.

⁴³ Davis, *Exorcism*, pp. 13, 14.

⁴⁴ Dickason, *Possession*, p. 187.

⁴⁵ Culpepper, *Charismatic Movement*, pp. 136–37.

⁴⁶ Baker, "Possession and the Occult," p. 248.

⁴⁷ Erickson, *Christian Theology*, 1:450.

⁴⁸ Davis, *Exorcism*, p. 10.

⁴⁹ See John Warwick Montgomery, ed., *Demon Possession: A Medical, Historical, Anthropological and Theological Symposium* (Minneapolis, MN: Bethany Fellowship, 1976).

⁵⁰ William Hendricksen, *Exposition of the Pastoral Epistles*, NTC (Grand Rapids: Baker Book House, 1957), p. 301.

⁵¹ Ibid., p. 305.

⁵² Erickson, *Christian Theology*, 1:202.

⁵³ Alva J. McClain, syllabus for the course "Christian Theology: God and Revelation," revised by John C. Whitcomb, Jr., and Ivan H. French, Grace Theological Seminary, Winona Lake, IN, n.d., p. 126.

⁵⁴ Jay E. Adams, *The Christian Counselor's Manual* (Phillipsburg, NJ: Presbyterian and Reformed Publishing Company, 1973), pp. 93, 94.

⁵⁵ Ibid., p. 94.

[56] Abbott-Smith, *Lexicon*, p. 61.

[57] Kenneth S. Wuest, "The Pastoral Epistles in the Greek New Testament," vol. 2 in *Wuest's Word Studies from the Greek New Testament*, 4 vols. (Grand Rapids: Wm. B. Eerdmans Publishing Co., 1966), p. 151.

[58] Moulton and Milligan, *Vocabulary*, p. 222.

[59] TDNT, s.v. "*artios*," by Gerhard Delling, 1:475–76.

[60] Dave Hunt, *Beyond Seduction: A Return to Biblical Christianity* (Eugene, OR: Harvest House Publishers, 1987), p. 126.

[61] Adams, *Counselor's Manual*, p. 97.

[62] Bufford, *Counseling*, pp. 111–15.

[63] Ibid., p. 115.

[64] Dickason, *Possession*, p. 187.

[65] Ibid., p. 148.

[66] Ibid., pp. 127, 147, 157.

[67] Ibid., p. 158.

[68] Ibid., pp. 153–60.

[69] Ibid., pp. 227, 28.

[70] Ibid., p. 233.

[71] Ibid., p. 237.

[72] Bubeck, *The Adversary*, pp. 93, 94.

[73] Dickason, *Possession*, pp. 307, 309.

[74] Ibid., p. 313.

[75] Ibid., pp. 190, 197–98. See also Ensign and Howe, *Supernatural Healing*, pp. 150–51.

[76] Ibid., p. 281.

CHAPTER 6

[1] BAGD, p. 500.

[2] Ibid.

[3] James L. Boyer, notes for the course, "Greek Exegesis: Ephesians," revised (Winona Lake, IN: Grace Theological Seminary, 1975), p. 63.

[4] Kenneth S. Wuest, "Ephesians and Colossians in the Greek New Testament," in vol. 1 of *Wuest's Word Studies from the Greek New Testament*, 4 vols. (Grand Rapids: Wm. B. Eerdmans Publishing Co., 1966), p. 141.

[5] TDNT, s.v. "*kratos*," by Wilhelm Michaelis, 3:905–6.

[6] Ibid., 3:914.

[7] David L. Warren, "A Biblical Study of the Phrase, 'Put on Christ'" (Th.M. thesis, Dallas Theological Seminary, May 1973), pp. 9, 46.

[8] TDNT, s.v. "*enduō*," by Albrecht Oepke, 2:319.

[9] For the historical description of the appearance and function of the Roman soldier's armor, the author is indebted to James L. Boyer, "Greek Exegesis: Ephesians" (course notes, Grace Theological Seminary, 1974), pp. 81–84.

[10] BAGD, pp. 13, 14.

[11] Bruce, *Acts*, pp. 391–92, 397–98.

BIBLIOGRAPHY

Abbott-Smith, G. *A Manual Greek Lexicon of the New Testament*. New York: Charles Scribner's Sons, 1921.

Adams, Jay E. *The Christian Counselor's Manual*. Phillipsburg, NJ: Presbyterian and Reformed Publishing Company, 1973.

Aland, Kurt, Matthew Black, Carol M. Martini, Bruce M. Metzger, and Allen Wickgren, eds. *The Greek New Testament*. 2nd ed. New York: United Bible Societies, 1966.

Alexander, William Menzies. *Demonic Possession in the New Testament: Its Relations—Historical, Medical, and Theological*. Edinburgh: T. & T. Clark, 1902.

Allen, Willoughby C. *A Critical and Exegetical Commentary on the Gospel According to St. Matthew*. ICC. Edinburgh: T. & T. Clark, 1907.

Baker, M. J. "Possession and the Occult—A Psychiatrist's View." *Churchman* 94 (May 1980): 246–53.

Barnes, Albert. *James, Peter, John and Jude*. In vol. 10 of *Barnes' Notes on the New Testament*. 11 vols. London: Blackie and Son, n.d.

Bartlett, David Lyon. "Exorcism Stories in the Gospel of Mark." Ph.D. dissertation, Yale University, 1972.

Basham, Don. *Deliver Us from Evil*. Washington Depot, CT: Chosen Books, 1972.

Bauer, Walter, William F. Arndt, and F. Wilbur Gingrich. *A Greek-English Lexicon of the New Testament and Other Early Christian Literature*. 2nd ed., revised and augmented by F. Wilbur Gingrich and Frederick W. Danker. Chicago: The University of Chicago Press, 1979.

Baxter, Ronald E. *Gifts of the Spirit*. Grand Rapids: Kregel Publications, 1983.

Berends, Willem. "The Biblical Criteria for Demon Possession." *The Westminster Theological Journal* 37 (Spring 1975): 342–65.

Bonnell, John Sutherland. "Jesus and Demon Possession." *Theology Today* 13 (July 1956): 208–19.

Bowman, John. *The Gospel of Mark: The New Christian Jewish Passover Haggadah*. Leiden: E. J. Brill, 1965.

Boyer, James L. Notes for the course, "Greek Exegesis: Ephesians." Grace Theological Seminary, Winona Lake, IN, revised 1974.

Brown, Francis, S. R. Driver, C. A. Briggs, eds. *A Hebrew and English Lexicon of the Old Testament*. Oxford: at the Clarendon Press, 1968.

Bruce, A. B. "Matthew." In vol. 1 of *Expositor's Greek Testament*. 4 vols. Edited by W. Robertson Nicoll. Reprint ed. Grand Rapids: Wm. B. Eerdmans Publishing Co., 1967.

Bruce, F. F. *Commentary on the Book of Acts*. NIC. Grand Rapids: Wm. B. Eerdmans Publishing Co., 1975.

———. *The Epistle to the Ephesians*. London: Pickering and Inglio, Ltd., 1961.

Brumbeck, Carl. *Suddenly from Heaven*. Springfield, MO: Gospel Publishing House, 1961.

Bubeck, Mark I. *The Adversary: The Christian Versus Demonic Activity*. Chicago: Moody Press, 1975.

———. *Overcoming the Adversary*. Chicago: Moody Press, 1984.

Bufford, Rodger K. *Counseling and the Demonic*. Resources for Christian Counseling. Edited by Gary R. Collins. Dallas: Word Books, 1988.

Buswell, James Oliver. *A Systematic Theology of the Christian Religion*. One volume ed., reprinted. Grand Rapids: Zondervan Publishing House, 1981.

Buttrick, George Arthur, ed. *The Interpreter's Bible*. 12 vols. New York:

Abingdon Press, 1951.

Calvin, John. "The First Epistle General of John." In vol. 5 of *Calvin's New Testament Commentaries*. Translated by T. H. L. Parker, the translation edited by David W. Torrance and Thomas F. Torrance. Grand Rapids: Wm. B. Eerdmans Publishing Co., 1961.

Caneday, Ardel B. "The Significance and Relationship of the Laying On of Hands and the Bestowal of Spiritual Gifts." M.Div. thesis, Grace Theological Seminary, 1976.

Chadwick, G. A. "Some Cases of Possession." *The Expositor*, 4th Series, 6 (1892): 272–81.

Chafer, Lewis Sperry. *Satan: His Motive and Methods*. New and revised ed., reprinted. Chicago: Moody Press, 1918.

———. Systematic *Theology*. 7 vols. Dallas: Dallas Seminary Press, 1947.

Cortes, Juan B. and Florence M. Gatti. *The Case against Possession and Exorcisms*. New York: Vantage Press, 1975.

Cranfield, C. E. B. *The Gospel According to St. Mark*. 4th edition, revised. Cambridge: Cambridge University Press, 1972.

Culpepper, Robert H. *Evaluating the Charismatic Movement: A Theological and Biblical Appraisal*. Valley Forge, PA: Judson Press, 1977.

Dana, H. E. and Julius R. Mantey. *A Manual Grammar of the Greek New Testament*. New York: The MacMillan Company, 1927.

Davis, John J. *Demons, Exorcism and the Evangelical*. Winona Lake, IN: BMH Books, 1977.

Davis, Tom. Review of *Demon Possession and the Christian: A New Perspective* by C. Fred Dickason. *Grace Theological Journal* 10 (Spring 1989): 89–94.

Denton, W. *Commentary on the Acts of the Apostles*. London: George Bell and Sons, 1876.

Dickason, C. Fred. *Demon Possession and the Christian: A New Perspective*.

Chicago: Moody Press, 1987.

Dow, Graham. "The Case for the Existence of Demons." *Churchman* 94 (May 1980): 199–209.

Dunn, James G. D. and Graham H. Twelftree. "Demon-Possession and Exorcism in the New Testament." *Churchman* 94 (May 1980): 210–25.

Ebon, Martin. *The Devil's Bride: Exorcism Past and Present.* New York: Harper & Row, Publishers, 1974.

Edersheim, Alfred. *The Life and Times of Jesus the Messiah.* 1 vol. ed. Grand Rapids: Wm. B. Eerdmans Publishing Co., 1971.

Edgar, Thomas R. "The Cessation of the Sign-Gifts," *Bibliotheca Sacra* 145 (October-December 1988): 371–86.

Ensign, Grayson H. and Edward Howe. *Bothered? Bewildered? Bewitched? Your Guide to Practical Supernatural Healing.* Cincinnati, OH: Recovery Publishers, 1984.

Erdman, Charles R. *The Epistle of Paul to the Ephesians: An Exposition.* Philadelphia: The Westminster Press, 1981.

Erickson, Millard J. *Christian Theology.* 1 vol. Grand Rapids: Baker Book House, 1983.

Findlay, G. G. *Fellowship in the Life Eternal.* London: Hodder and Stoughton, 1909.

Foulkes, Francis. *The Epistle of Paul to the Ephesians: An Introduction and Commentary.* Tyndale New Testament Commentaries. Grand Rapids: Wm. B. Eerdmans Publishing Co., 1963.

Fridrichsen, Anton. "The Conflict of Jesus with Unclean Spirits." *Theology: A Journal of Historic Christianity* 22 (March 1931): 122–35.

Gangel, Kenneth O. *You and Your Spiritual Gifts.* Chicago: Moody Press, 1975.

Geldenhuys, Norval. *Commentary on the Gospel of Luke.* NIC. Grand

Rapids: Wm. B. Eerdmans Publishing Co., 1979.

———. *Supreme Authority: The Authority of the Lord, His Apostles and the New Testament*. Grand Rapids: Wm. B. Eerdmans Publishing Co., 1953.

Godet, F. *Commentary on the First Epistle of St. Paul to the Corinthians*. Translated by A. Cusin. 2 vols. Edinburgh: T. & T. Clark, 1886; reprint ed., Grand Rapids: Zondervan Publishing House, 1957.

Gore, Tipper. *Raising PG Kids in an X-Rated Society*. Nashville: Abingdon Press. 1987.

Gromacki, Robert Glenn. *The Modern Tongues Movement*. Philadelphia, PA: Presbyterian and Reformed Publishing Co., 1967.

———. *New Testament Survey*. Grand Rapids: Baker Book House, 1974.

Grosheide, F. W. *Commentary on the First Epistle to the Corinthians*. NIC. Grand Rapids: Wm. B. Eerdmans Publishing Co., 1953.

Habershon, Ada R. *The Study of the Miracles*. Grand Rapids: Kregel Publications, 1957.

Hagin, Kenneth E. *The Satan, Demons, and Demon Possession Series*. 4 vol. Tulsa, OK: Kenneth Hagin Ministries, 1983.

Harper, Michael. *Spiritual Warfare: Recognizing and Overcoming the Work of Evil Spirits*. Ann Arbor, MI: Servant Books, 1984.

Harrison, Everett F. *Introduction to the New Testament*. Grand Rapids: Wm. B. Eerdmans Publishing Co., 1964.

Haupt, Erich. *The First Epistle of John*. Translated by W. B. Pope. Edinburgh: T. & T. Clark, 1879.

Hearn, Daniel A. "Demonology and the Believer." M.Div. thesis, Grace Theological Seminary, 1978.

Hendricksen, William. *Exposition of the Gospel According to Mark*. NTC. Grand Rapids: Baker Book House, 1975.

————. *Exposition of the Gospel According to Matthew.* NTC. Grand Rapids: Baker Book House, 1973.

————. *Exposition of the Pastoral Epistles.* NTC. Grand Rapids: Baker Book House, 1957.

Hiebert, D. Edmond. *Mark: A Portrait of the Servant.* Chicago: Moody Press, 1974.

Hiers, Richard H. *The Historical Jesus and the Kingdom of God.* Gainesville, FL: University of Florida Press, 1973.

————. *The Kingdom of God in the Synoptic Traditions.* University of Florida Humanities Monograph Number 3. Gainesville, FL: University of Florida Press, 1970.

————. "Satan, Demons and the Kingdom of God." *Scottish Journal of Theology* 27 (February 1974): 35–47.

Hitt, Russell F. *Demons, the Bible and You.* Newton, PA: Timothy Books, 1974.

Hodge, A. A. *Outlines in Theology.* New York: A. C. Armstrong and Son, 1891.

Hodge, Charles. *Commentary on the Epistle to the Ephesians.* Reprint ed., Evangelical Masterworks Series. Old Tappan, NJ: Fleming H. Revell Company, n.d.

————. *An Exposition of the First Epistle to the Corinthians.* Grand Rapids: Wm. B. Eerdmans Publishing Co., 1950.

————. *Systematic Theology.* 3 vols. New York: Scribner, Armstrong and Co., 1872.

Hunt, Dave. *Beyond Seduction: A Return to Biblical Christianity.* Eugene, OR: Harvest House Publishers, 1987.

Hunt, Dave and T. A. McMahon. *The Seduction of Christianity: Spiritual Discernment in the Last Days.* Eugene, OR: Harvest House Publishers, 1985.

Ironside, H. A. *Addresses on the First Epistle to the Corinthians.* Neptune, NJ: Loizeaux Brothers, 1938.

———. *The Epistle of John.* New York: Loizeaux Brothers, 1945.

Jacobs, Donald. *Demons: An Examination of Demons at Work in the World Today.* Scottsdale, PA: Herald Press, 1972.

Josephus. *Antiquities of the Jews.*

Kee, Howard Clark. "The Terminology of Mark's Exorcism Stories." *New Testament Studies* 14 (January 1968): 232–46.

Kemp, William C. "Did Jesus Cast Out Demons? Mark 12:27." B.D. monograph, Grace Theological Seminary, 1960.

Kent, Homer A., Jr. *Ephesians: The Glory of the Church.* Chicago, Moody Press, 1971.

———. *The Epistle to the Hebrews.* Winona Lake, IN: BMH Books, 1972.

———. *The Freedom of God's Sons: Studies in Galatians.* Winona Lake, IN: BMH Books, 1976.

———. *Jerusalem to Rome: Studies in the Book of Acts.* Winona Lake, IN: BMH Books, 1972.

———. *Studies in the Gospel of Mark.* Winona Lake, IN: BMH Books, 1981.

Ketcham, Robert T. *God's Provision for Normal Christian Living.* Moody Pocket Book Edition. Chicago: Moody Press, 1963.

Koch, Kurt E. *Between Christ and Satan.* Grand Rapids: Kregel Publications, 1973.

———. *Demonology Past and Present.* Grand Rapids: Kregel Publications, 1973.

———. *The Devil's Alphabet.* Grand Rapids: Kregel Publications, 1971.

———. *Occult Bondage and Deliverance: Advice for Counseling the Sick, the*

Troubled, and the Occultly Oppressed. Grand Rapids: Kregel Publications, 1971.

Konya, Alex W. "Demons: Wandering, Seeking, Returning." Paper presented for the Theology Seminar: "The Teachings of Jesus," Grace Theological Seminary, Winona Lake, IN, October 1975.

————. "The Meaning of the Trial of the Spirits in 1 John 4:1–3." Paper prepared for the course "God and the World," at Grace Theological Seminary, Winona Lake, IN, July 1975.

Ladd, George Eldon. *Jesus and the Kingdom: The Eschatology of Biblical Realism.* New York: Harper & Row, Publishers, 1964.

Lane, William F. *The Gospel According to Mark.* NIC. Grand Rapids: Wm. B. Eerdmans Publishing Co., 1974.

Lange, John Peter. "The First Epistle General of John." In vol. 23 of *Commentary on the Holy Scriptures.* Translated and edited by Philip Schaff. Grand Rapids: Zondervan Publishing House, n.d.

Langton, Edward. *Essentials of Demonology.* London: The Epworth Press, 1949.

Lenski, R. C. H. *The Interpretation of the Acts of the Apostles.* Reprint ed. Minneapolis, MN: Augsburg Publishing House, 1964.

————. *The Interpretation of the Epistles of St. Peter, St. John and St. Jude.* Reprint ed. Minneapolis, MN: Augsburg Publishing House, 1966.

————. *The Interpretation of St. Mark's Gospel.* Reprint ed. Minneapolis, MN: Augsburg Publishing House, 1964.

————. *The Interpretation of St. Matthew's Gospel.* Reprint ed. Minneapolis, MN: Augsburg Publishing House, 1967.

————. *The Interpretation of St. Paul's Epistles to the Galatians, to the Ephesians and to the Philippians.* Reprint ed. Minneapolis, MN: Augsburg Publishing House, 1961.

————. *The Interpretation of St. Paul's First and Second Epistles to the*

Corinthians. Reprint ed. Minneapolis, MN: Augsburg Publishing House, 1963.

Lhermitte, Jacques Jean. *Diabolical Possession, True and False*. Translated by P. J. Hepburne-Scott. London: Burns & Oates, 1963.

Lightner, Robert P. Review of *Demons in the World Today*, by Merrill F. Unger. *Bibliotheca Sacra* 129 (July-September 1972): 264.

Linn, Matthew and Dennis. *Deliverance Prayer: Experiential, Psychological and Theological Approaches*. New York: Paulist Press, 1981.

Luce, H. K. "The Gospel According to St. Luke." In *The Cambridge Greek Testament for Schools and Colleges*. Edited by A. Nairne. Cambridge: The Cambridge University Press, 1949.

MacArthur, John F., Jr. *The Charismatics: A Doctrinal Perspective*. Grand Rapids: Zondervan Publishing House, 1978.

Macaulay, J. *Behold Your King*. Chicago: Moody Press, 1982.

McClain, Alva J. *The Greatness of the Kingdom*. Winona Lake, IN: BMH Books, 1974.

————. Syllabus for the course "Christian Theology: God and Revelation." Revised by John C. Whitcomb, Jr., and Ivan H. French. Grace Theological Seminary, Winona Lake, IN, n.d.

————. Syllabus for the course "Christian Theology: God and the Word." Revised by Charles R. Smith. Grace Theological Seminary, Winona Lake, IN, 1975.

————. Syllabus for the course "Christian Theology: Salvation and the Christian Life." Revised by John C. Whitcomb, Jr., and Charles R. Smith. Grace Theological Seminary, Winona Lake, IN, n.d.

MacMillan, A. J. *Modern Demon Possession*. Harrisburg, PA: Christian Publications, Inc., n.d.

Mallone, George. *Those Controversial Gifts*. Downer's Grove, IL: Inter-Varsity Press, 1983.

Masters, Peter. *The Healing Epidemic*. London: The Wakeman Trust, 1988.

Masters, Peter and John C. Whitcomb, Jr. *The Charismatic Phenomenon*. London: The Metropolitan Tabernacle, Elephant & Castle, 1982.

Mayer, John Russell. "In My Name Shall They Cast Out Demons Mark, 16:17." B.D. monograph, Grace Theological Seminary, 1968.

Meigs, J. Thomas. "Pastoral Care Methods and Demonology in Selected Writings." *Journal of Psychology and Theology* 5 (Summer 1977): 234–46.

Montgomery, John Warwick, ed. *Demon Possession: A Medical, Historical, Anthropological and Theological Symposium*. Minneapolis, MN: Bethany Fellowship, 1976.

———. "Exorcism: Is it for Real?" *Christianity Today*, July 26, 1974: 5–8.

Morgan, G. Campbell. *The Gospel According to Matthew*. New York: Fleming H. Revell Co., 1929.

———. *The Gospel According to Mark*. Old Tappan, NJ: Fleming H. Revell Co., 1927.

Moule, H. C. G. *Studies in Ephesians*. The Cambridge Bible for Schools and Colleges. At the University Press, 1893; reprint ed., Grand Rapids: Kregel Popular Commentary Series, 1977.

Moulton, James Hope and George Milligan. *The Vocabulary of the Greek Testament Illustrated from the Papyri and Other Non-Literary Sources*. Grand Rapids: Wm. B. Eerdmans Publishing Co., 1930.

Nauman, St. Elmo, ed. *Exorcism through the Ages*. New York: Philosophical Library, 1974.

Nelson, Marion H. *Why Christians Crack Up*. Chicago: Moody Press, 1967.

Nevius, John L. *Demon Possession and Allied Themes*. 5th edition. New York: Fleming H. Revell Co., n.d.

New International Dictionary of New Testament Theology. S.v. "*ekballō*," by Hans Bietenhard.

————. S.v. "*exorkistes*," by J. Stafford Wright.

Pentecost, J. Dwight. *Your Adversary the Devil.* Grand Rapids: Zondervan Publishing House, 1969.

Pereira, John. "Jewish Exorcism: a Harmonization of Matthew 12:27 and Acts 19:13–17." M.Div. thesis, Grace Theological Seminary, 1976.

Peterson, Robert. *Are Demons for Real?* Chicago: Moody Press, 1972.

Philpott, Kent. *A Manual for Demonology and the Occult.* Grand Rapids: Zondervan Publishing House, 1973.

Plummer, Alfred. *An Exegetical Commentary of the Gospel According to St. Matthew.* Grand Rapids: Wm B. Eerdmans Publishing Co., 1956.

Plumptre, E. H. "The Gospel According to St. Matthew, St. Mark, and St. Luke." In vol. 6 of *A Bible Commentary for English Readers.* Edited by John Ellicott. London: Casell and Co., n.d.

Robertson, Archibald Thomas. "The First Epistle of John." In vol. 6 of *Word Pictures in the New Testament.* 7 vols. New York: Harper and Brothers, Publishers, 1933.

————. *A Harmony of the Gospels for Students of the Life of Christ.* New York: Harper & Row, Publishers, 1922.

————. *Word Pictures in the New Testament.* 6 vols. Nashville, TN: Broadman Press, 1930.

Robinson, Theodore H. *The Gospel of Matthew.* London: Hodder and Stoughton, 1928.

Roosa, William V. "The Significance of Exorcism in the Gospel of Mark." Ph.D. dissertation, University of Chicago, 1934.

Runge, Albert. "Exorcism: A Satanic Ploy?" *His Dominion* 13:4 (1987): 123–19.

Sabourin, Leopold. "The Miracles of Jesus (II). Jesus and the Evil Powers." *Biblical Theology Bulletin* 4 (June 1974): 115–75.

Sall, Millard J. "Demon Possession or Psychopathology? A Clinical Differentiation." *Journal of Psychology and Theology* 4 (Fall 1976): 286–90.

Scaer, David P. *The Apostolic Scriptures*. St. Louis: Concordia Publishing House, 1971.

Schneider, Bernard H. *The World of Unseen Spirits—A Study Guide*. Winona Lake, IN: BMH Books, 1975.

Simpson, E. K., and Bruce, F. F. *Commentary on the Epistles to the Ephesians and the Colossians*. NIC. Grand Rapids: Wm. B. Eerdmans Publishing Co., 1980.

Scofield, C. I., ed. *The New Scofield Reference Bible*. New York: Oxford University Press, 1967.

Slaten, A. Wakefield. "Did Jesus Believe in Demons?" *Biblical World* 54 (July 1920): 371–77.

Smith, Charles R. "Biblical Conclusions Concerning Tongues." Th.D. dissertation, Grace Theological Seminary, May 1970.

———. "The New Testament Doctrine of Demons." *Grace Journal* 10 (Spring 1969): 32–42.

———. *Tongues in Biblical Perspective: A Summary of Biblical Conclusions Concerning Tongues*. 2nd edition (revised). Winona Lake, IN: BMH Books, 1973.

Strain, Robert Louis. "A Descriptive Study of the Phenomenon of Demon Possession from Selected Works of Kurt Koch." D.Min. dissertation, Fuller Theological Seminary, 1975.

Strong, Augustus Hopkins. *Systematic Theology*. 3 vols. in 1. Reprint ed. Valley Forge, PA: Judson Press, 1976.

Swete, Henry Barclay. *Commentary on Mark*. Grand Rapids: Kregel

Publications, 1977.

Taylor, E. Roger. "The Identity of the Spirits in 1 John 4:1." M.Div. thesis, Grace Theological Seminary, 1974.

Taylor, William M. *The Miracles of Our Savior Expounded and Illustrated.* 10th edition. New York: A. C. Armstrong & Son, 1910.

Tenney, Merrill C. "Luke." In *The Wycliffe Bible Commentary.* Edited by Charles F. Pfeiffer, and Everett F. Harrison. Chicago: Moody Press, 1962.

———. *New Testament Times.* Grand Rapids: Wm. B. Eerdmans Publishing Co., 1965.

Theological Dictionary of the New Testament. S.v. "*apostellō*," by Karl Heinrich Rengstorf.

———. S.v. "*artios*," by Gerhard Delling.

———. S.v. "*biazomai*," by Gottlob Schrenk.

———. S.v. "*daimōn, daimonion*," by Werner Foerster.

———. S.v. "*en*," by Albrecht Oepke.

———. S.v. "*epitimaō*," by Ethelbert Stauffer.

———. S.v. "*echō*," by Herman Hanse.

———. S.v. "*enduō*," by Albrecht Oepke.

———. S.v. "*iaomai*," by Albrecht Oepke.

———. S.v. "*kratos*," by Wilhelm Michaelis.

———. S.v. "*lambanō*," by Gerhard Delling.

———. S.v. "*sēmeion*," by Karl Heinrich Rengstorf.

Thayer, Henry Joseph. *Greek-English Lexicon of the New Testament.* New

York: American Book Co., 1889.

Thompson, Reginald Campbell. *The Devils and Evil Spirits of Babylonia.* New York: AMS Press, 1976.

Timmons, Tim. *Chains of the Spirit: A Manual for Liberation.* Washington, D.C.: Canon Press, 1973.

Travis, Arthur E. "The Christian's Warfare: An Exegetical Study of Ephesians Six (6:10–18)." *Southwestern Journal of Theology* 6 (October 1963): 71–80.

Trench, Richard Chenevix. *Notes on the Miracles of Our Lord.* Westwood, NJ: Fleming H. Revell Co., 1953.

————. *Synonyms of the New Testament.* Grand Rapids: Associated Publishers and Authors, Inc., n.d.

Unger, Merrill Frederick. *Biblical Demonology.* Wheaton, IL: Van Kampen Press, 1952.

————. *Demons in the World Today.* Wheaton, IL: Tyndale House Publishers, 1971.

————. *What Demons Can Do to Saints.* Chicago: Moody Press, 1977.

Vanderloos, H. *The Miracles of Jesus.* Leiden: E. J. Brill, 1965.

Vincent, M. R. "Matthew." In vol. 1 of *Word Studies in the New Testament.* 2 vols. MacDill AFB, FL: MacDonald Publishing Co., n.d.

Walvoord, John F. *The Holy Spirit.* Wheaton, IL: Van Kampen Press, 1954.

————. *The Holy Spirit at Work Today.* Chicago: Moody Press, 1973.

Warfield, Benjamin B. *Counterfeit Miracles.* New York: Charles Scribner's Sons, 1918.

Warren, David L. "A Biblical Study of the Phrase, 'Put On Christ.' " Th.M. thesis, Dallas Theological Seminary, May 1973.

Westcott, Brooke Foss. *The Epistles of St. John.* London: MacMillan and Company, 1886.

Wilson, Michael. "Exorcism: A Clinical/Pastoral Practice Which Raises Serious Questions." *Expository Times* 86 (July 1975): 292–95.

Wright, J. Stafford. *Christianity and the Occult.* Chicago: Moody Press, 1971.

Wuest, Kenneth S. "Ephesians and Colossians in the Greek New Testament." In vol. 1 of *Wuest's Word Studies from the Greek New Testament.* 4 vols. Grand Rapids: Wm. B. Eerdmans Publishing Co., 1966.

———. "In These Last Days." In vol. 4 of *Wuest's Word Studies from the Greek New Testament.* 4 vols. Grand Rapids: Wm. B. Eerdmans Publishing Co., 1966.

———. "The Pastoral Epistles in the Greek New Testament." In vol. 2 of *Wuest's Word Studies from the Greek New Testament.* 4 vols. Grand Rapids: Wm. B. Eerdmans Publishing Co., 1966.

Wycliffe Bible Encyclopedia, S.v. "Seventy Disciples of Our Lord."

Yates, Roy. "The Powers of Evil in the New Testament." *The Evangelical Quarterly* 52 (April—June 1980): 97–111.